For the little explorers of art and imagination, who color the world with the magic of their dreams. May each page of this coloring book be a colorful adventure, where creativity flies free and smiles are present in every stroke. May these blank pages be filled with joy, fun, and lots of colors, turning each moment into a unique and special masterpiece. May this book be an invitation to travel through imagination and discover a world full of endless possibilities. With love and gratitude.

Ana C. Espindula
2024

ALL RIGHTS RESERVERD
2024

All rights reserved. No part of this material may be reproduced, stored in a retrieval system, or transmitted in any form or by any means – electronic, mechanical, photocopying, recording, or otherwise – without prior written permission from the copyright holder.

A.C.E©

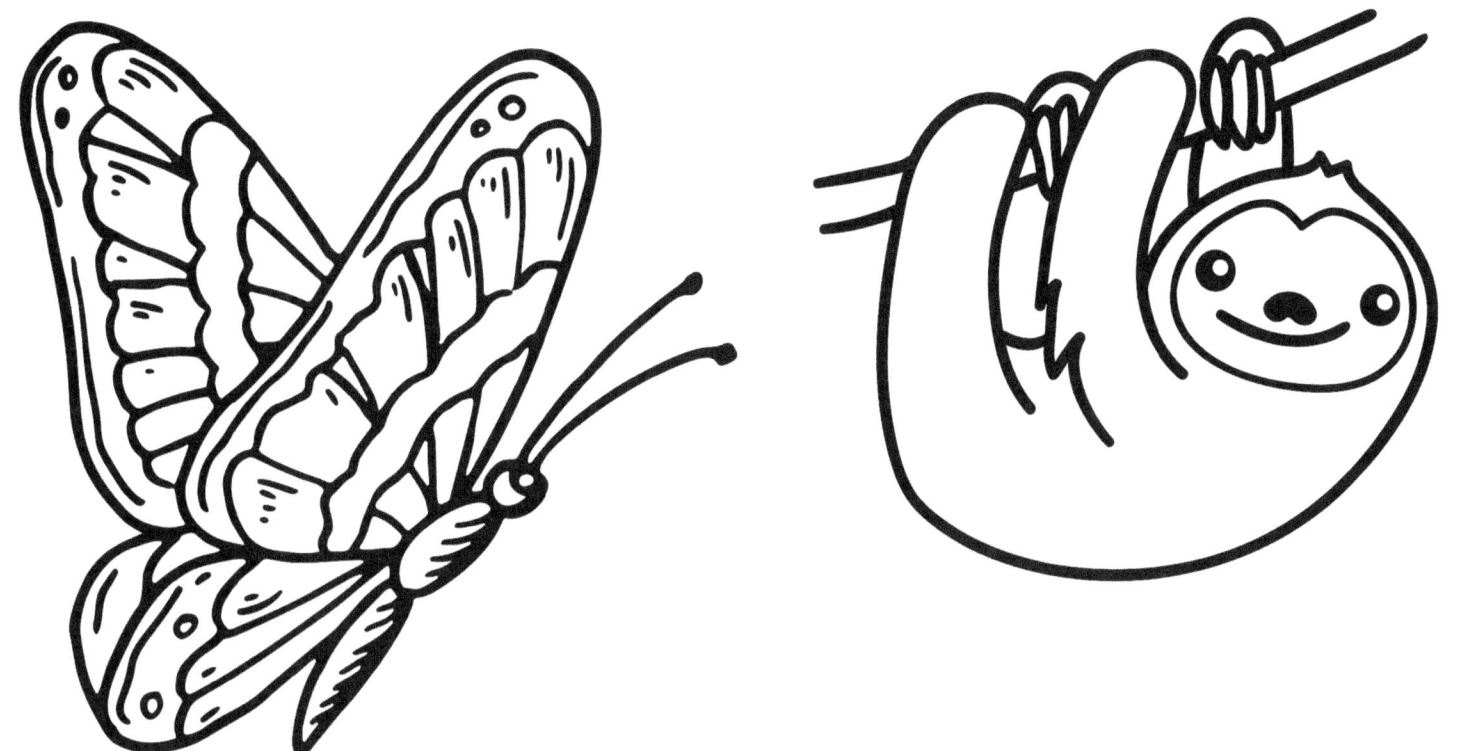

This Book Belongs Too:

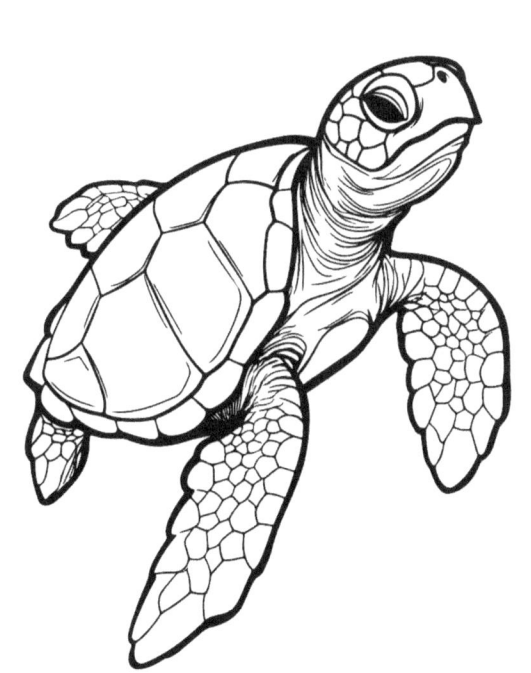

A.C.E©
rights reserved

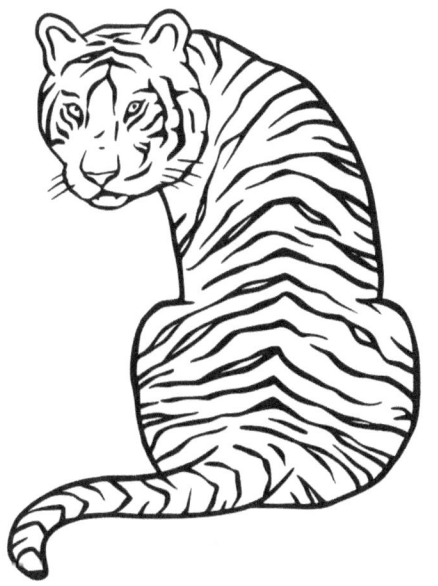

Test Color Page

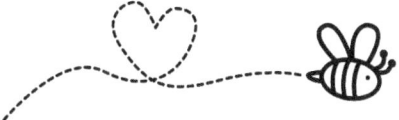

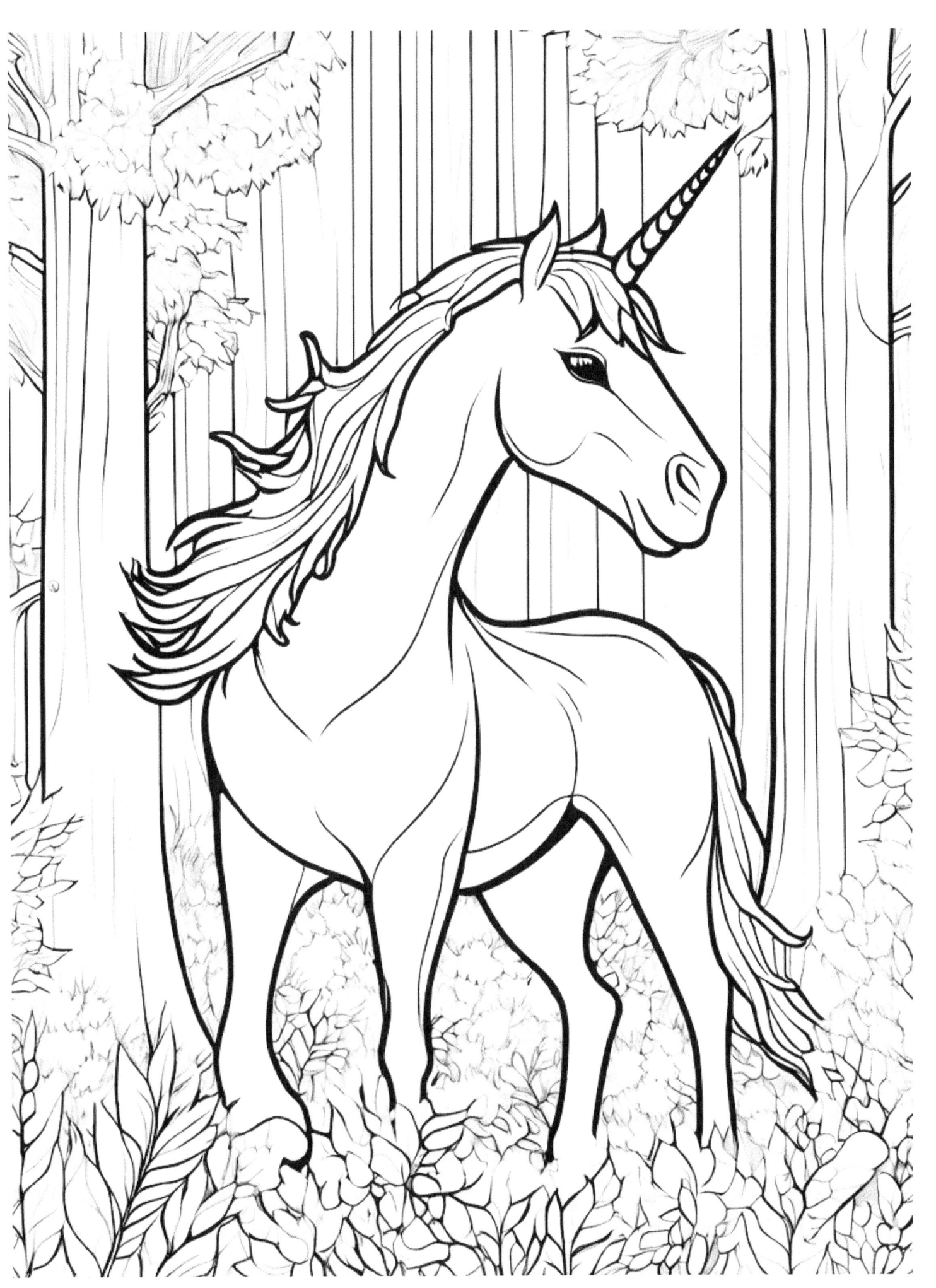

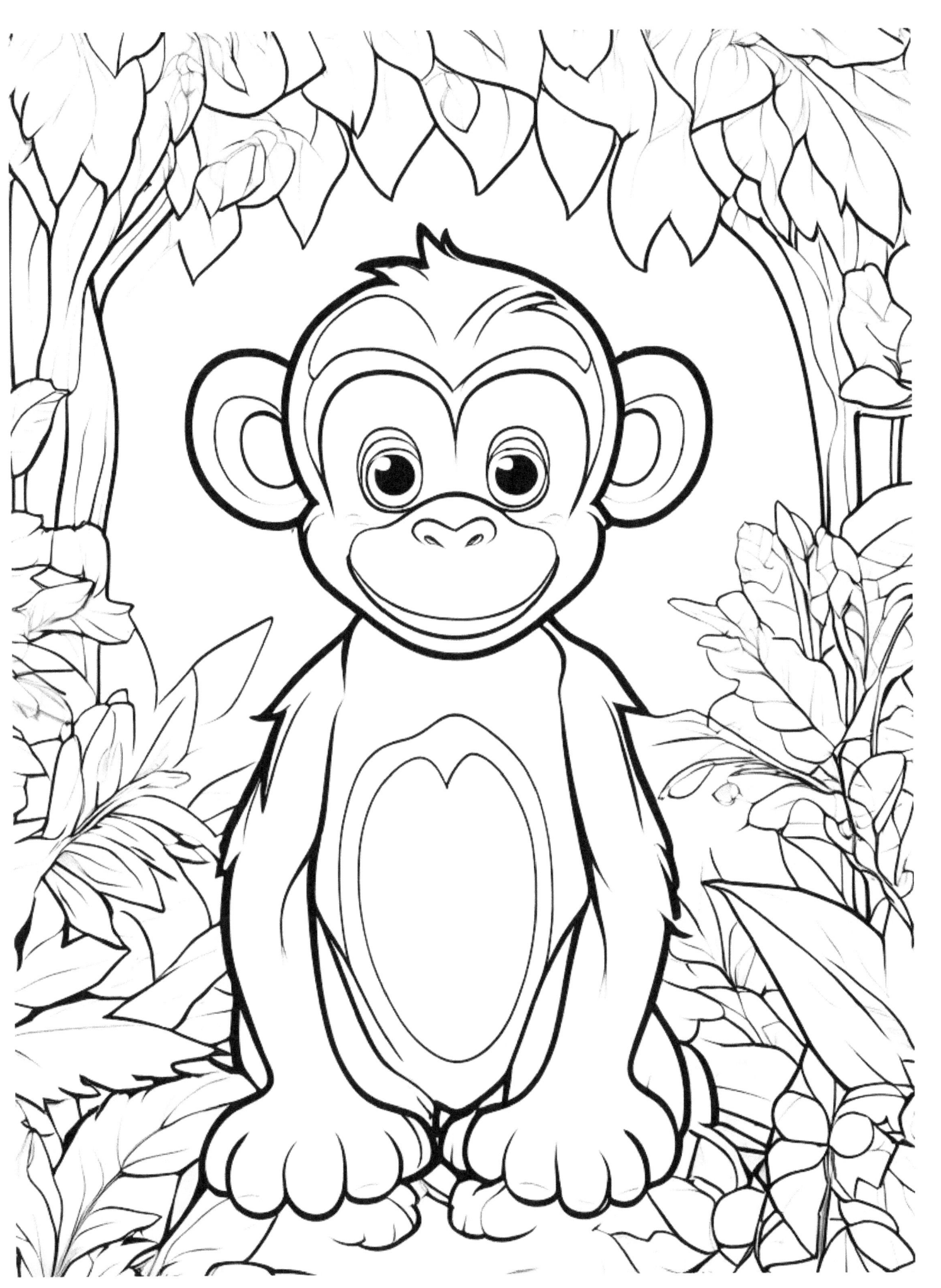

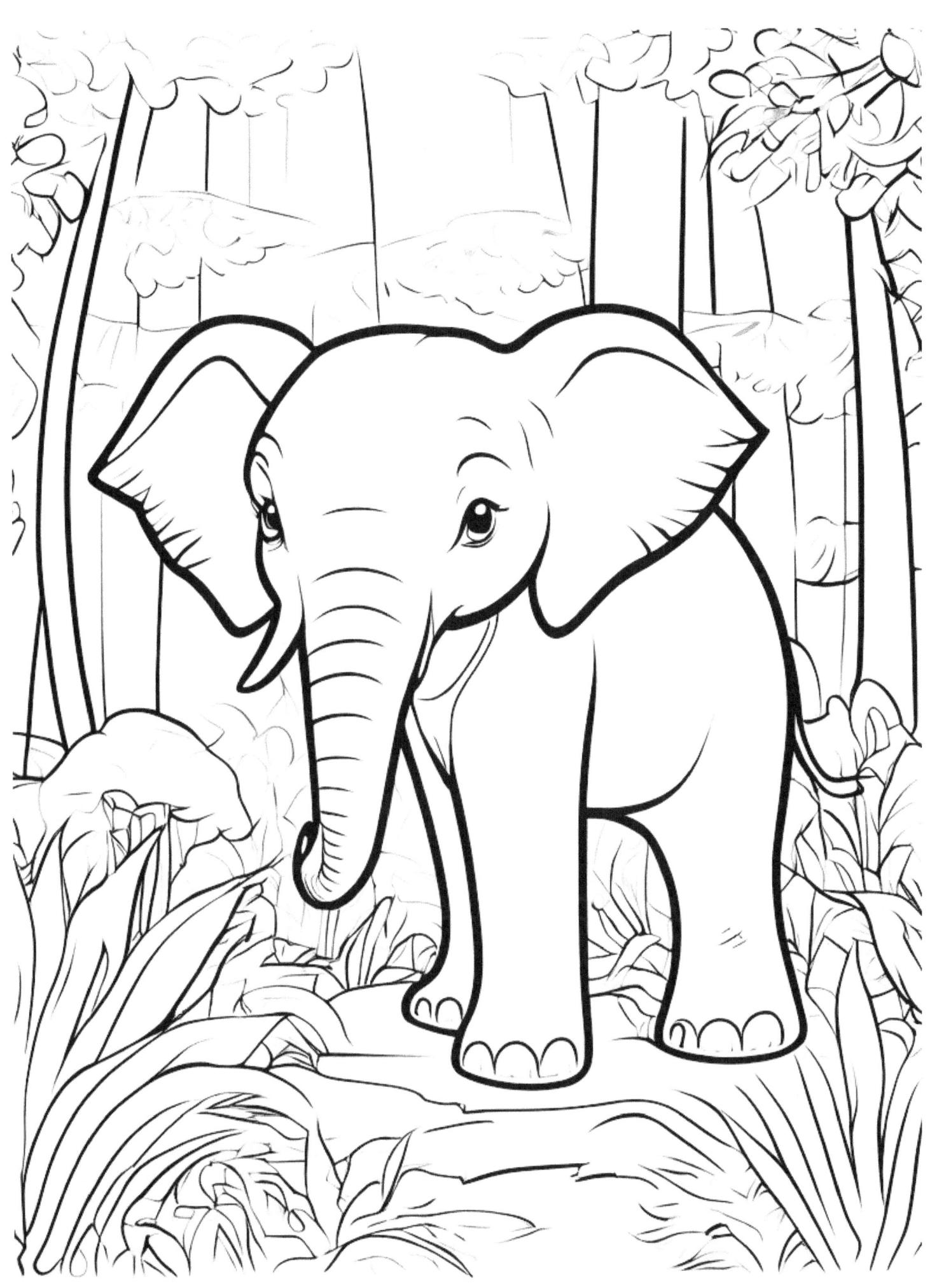

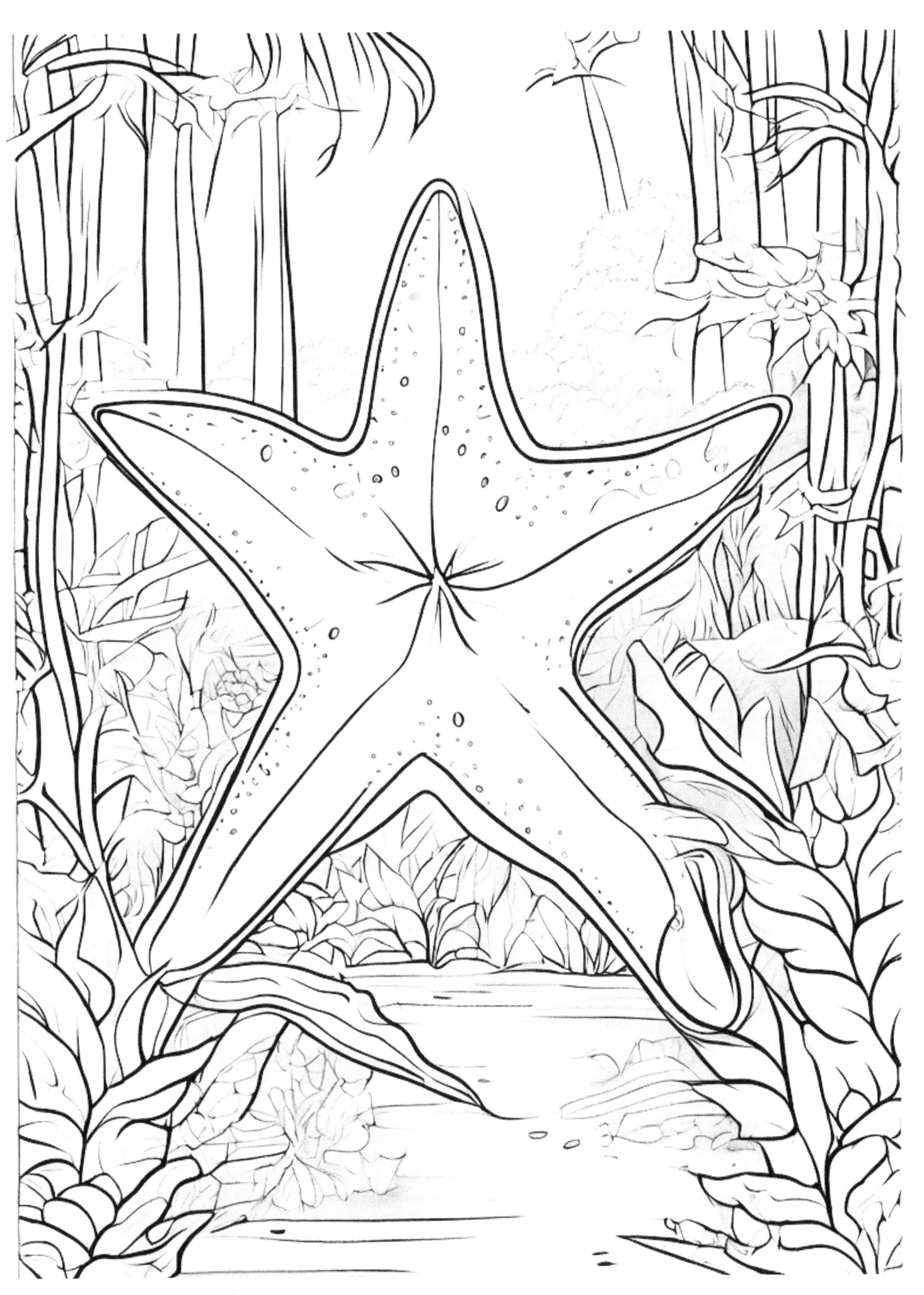

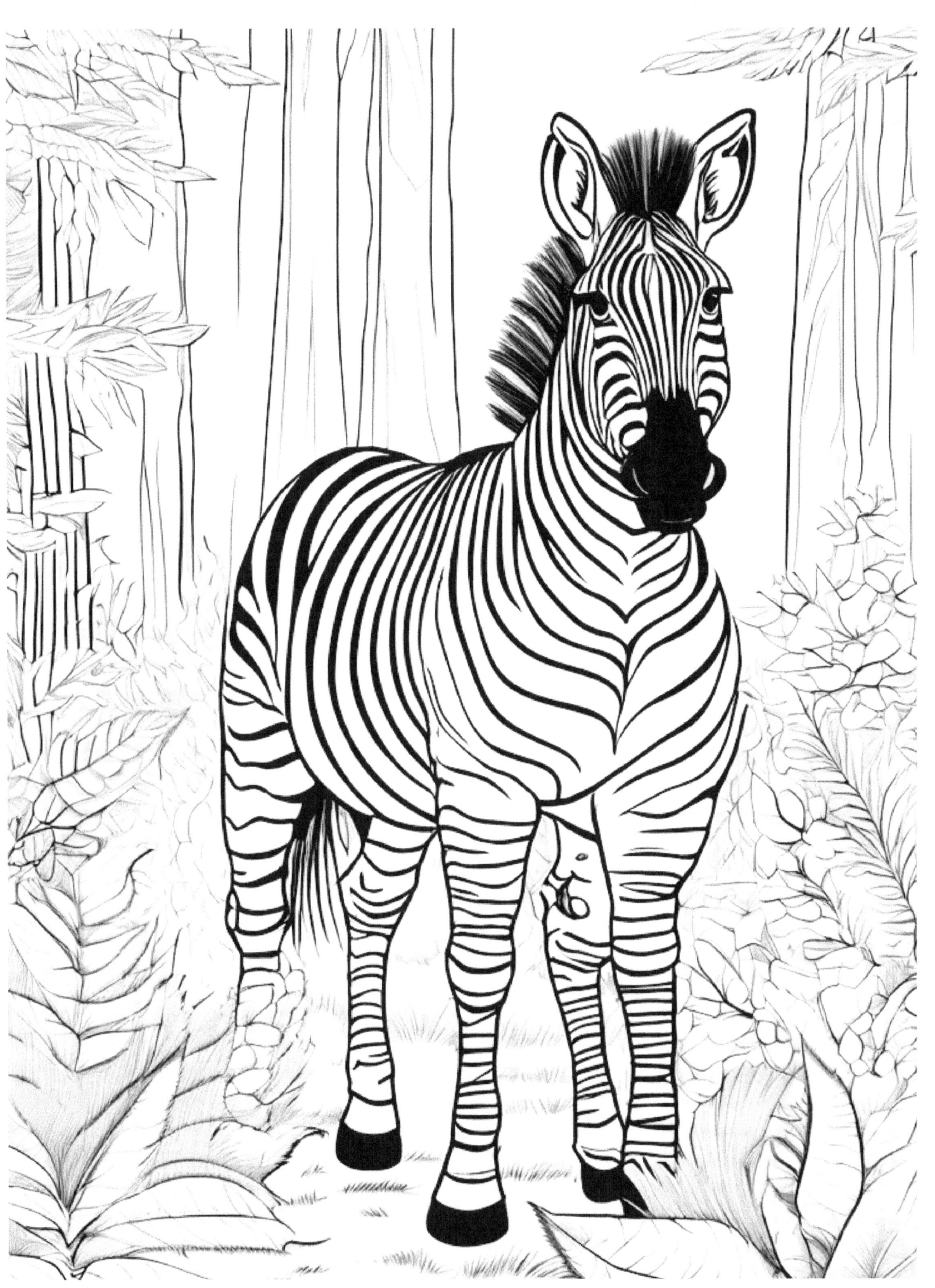

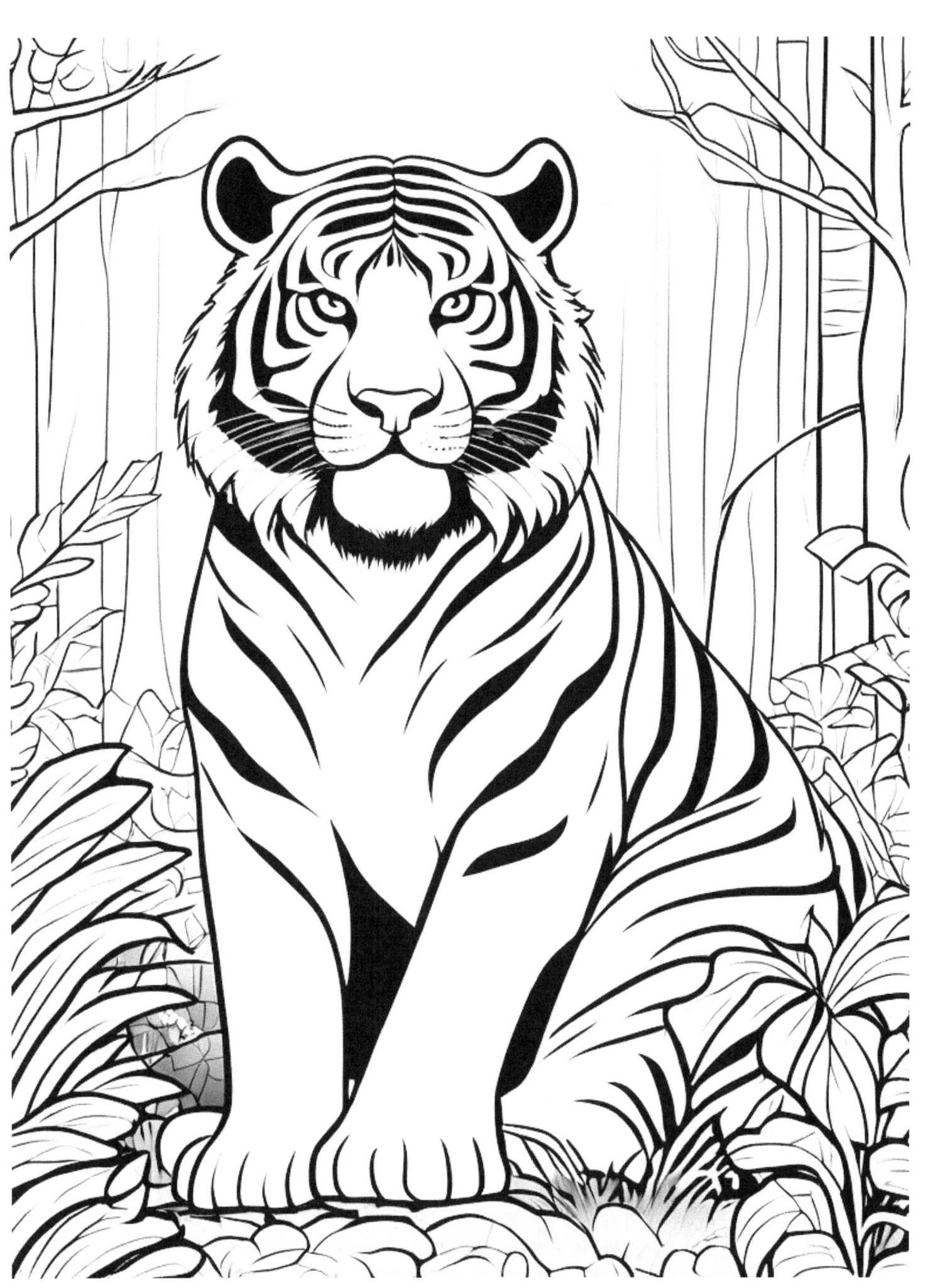

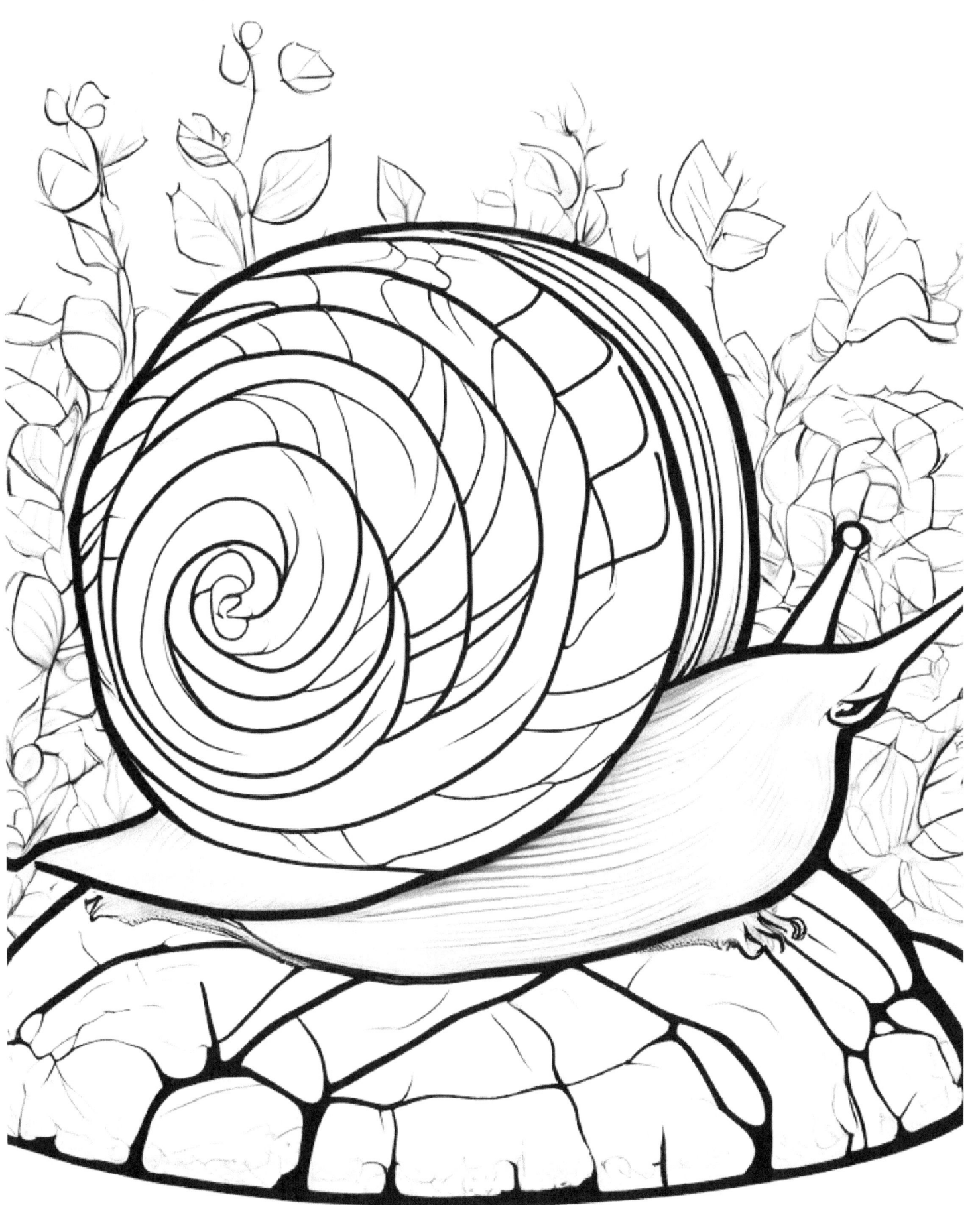

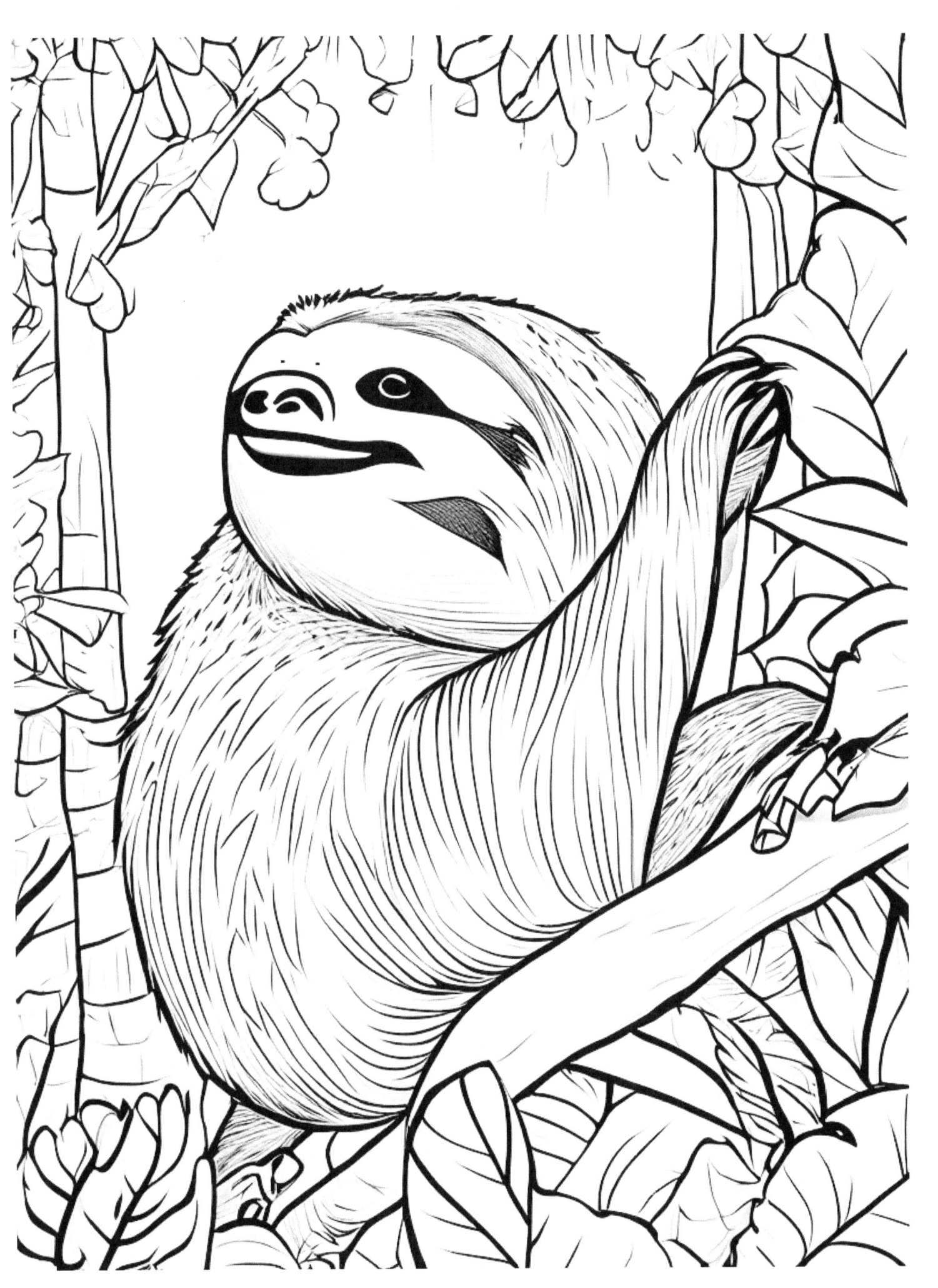

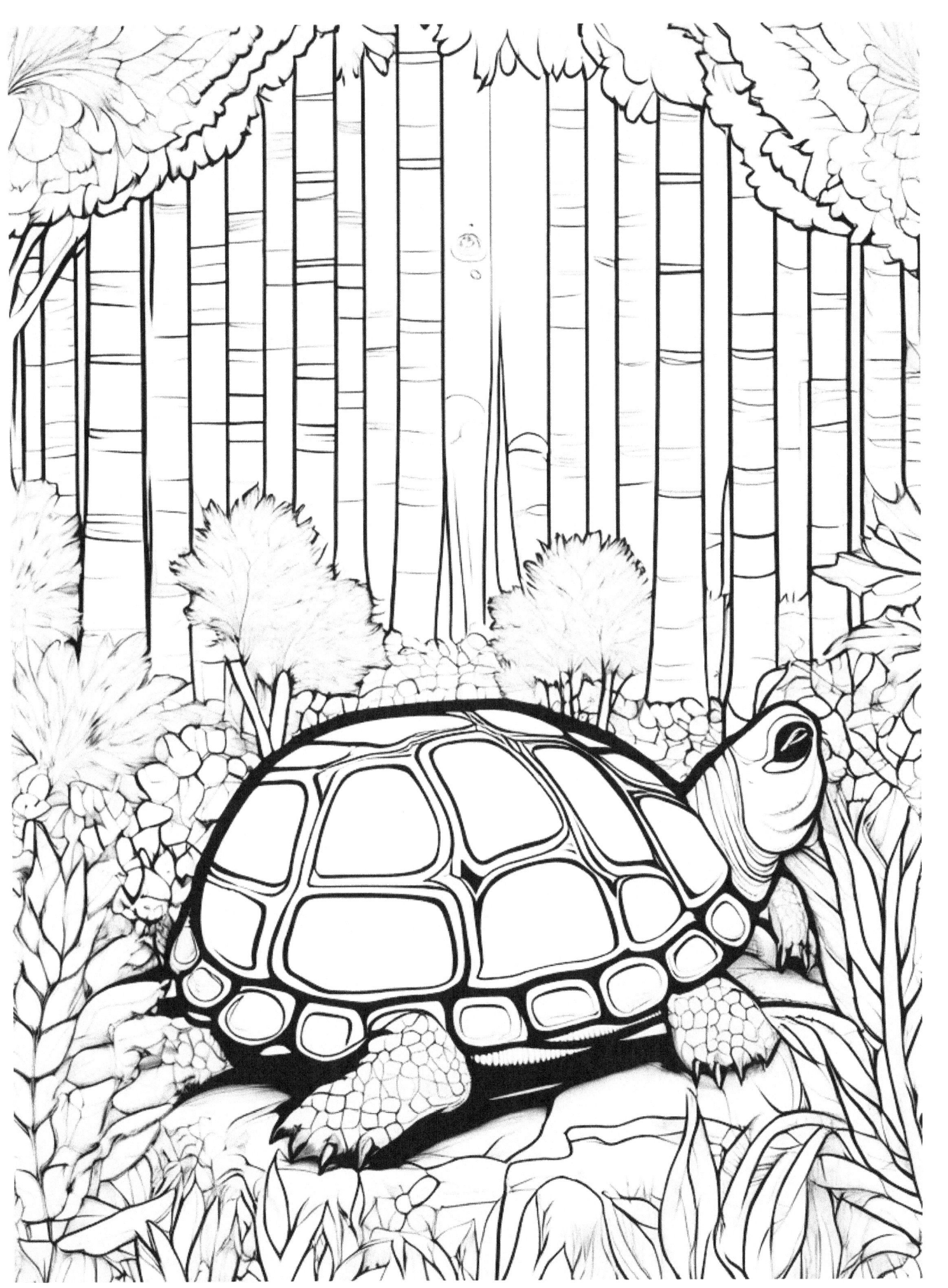

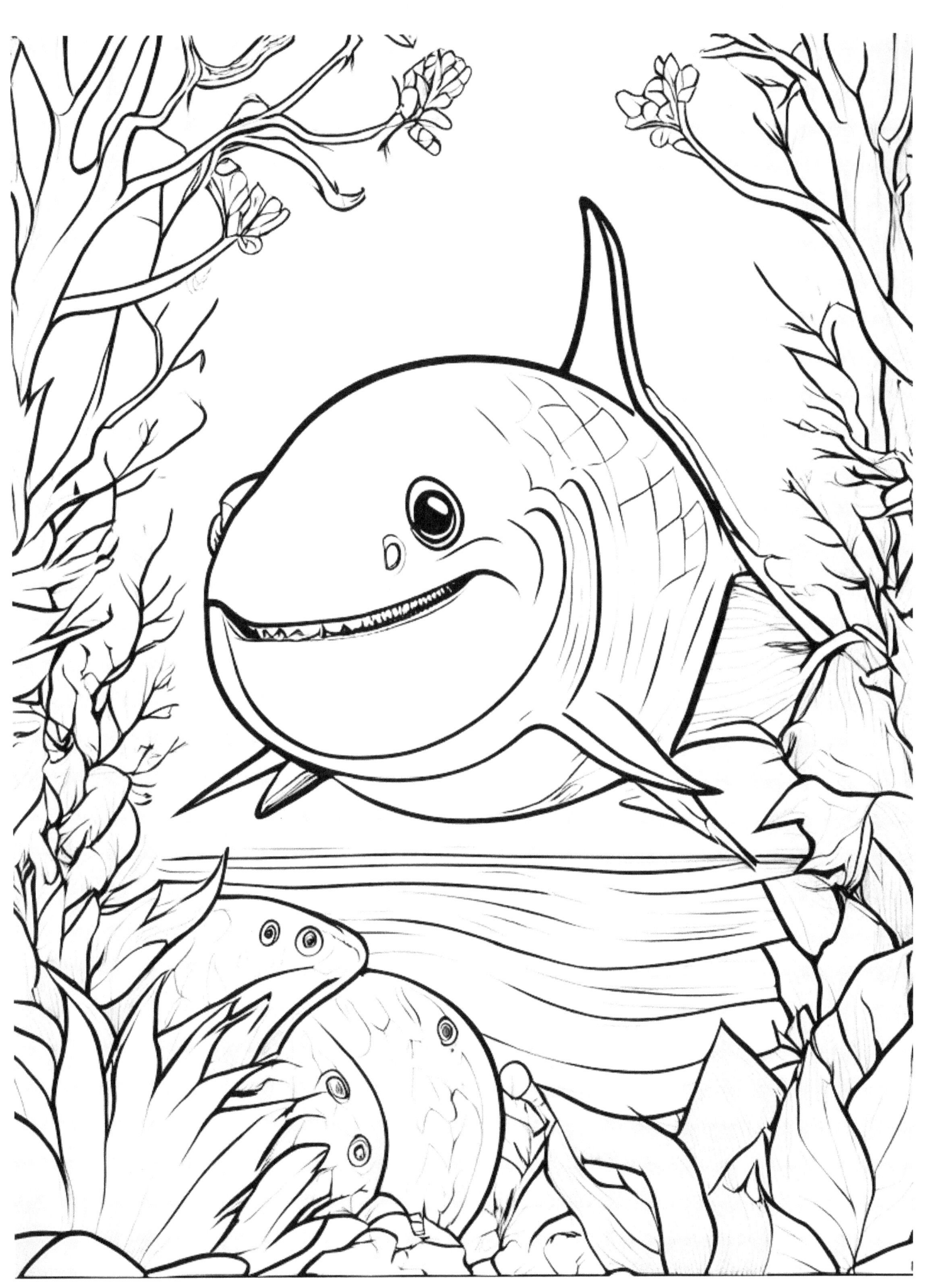

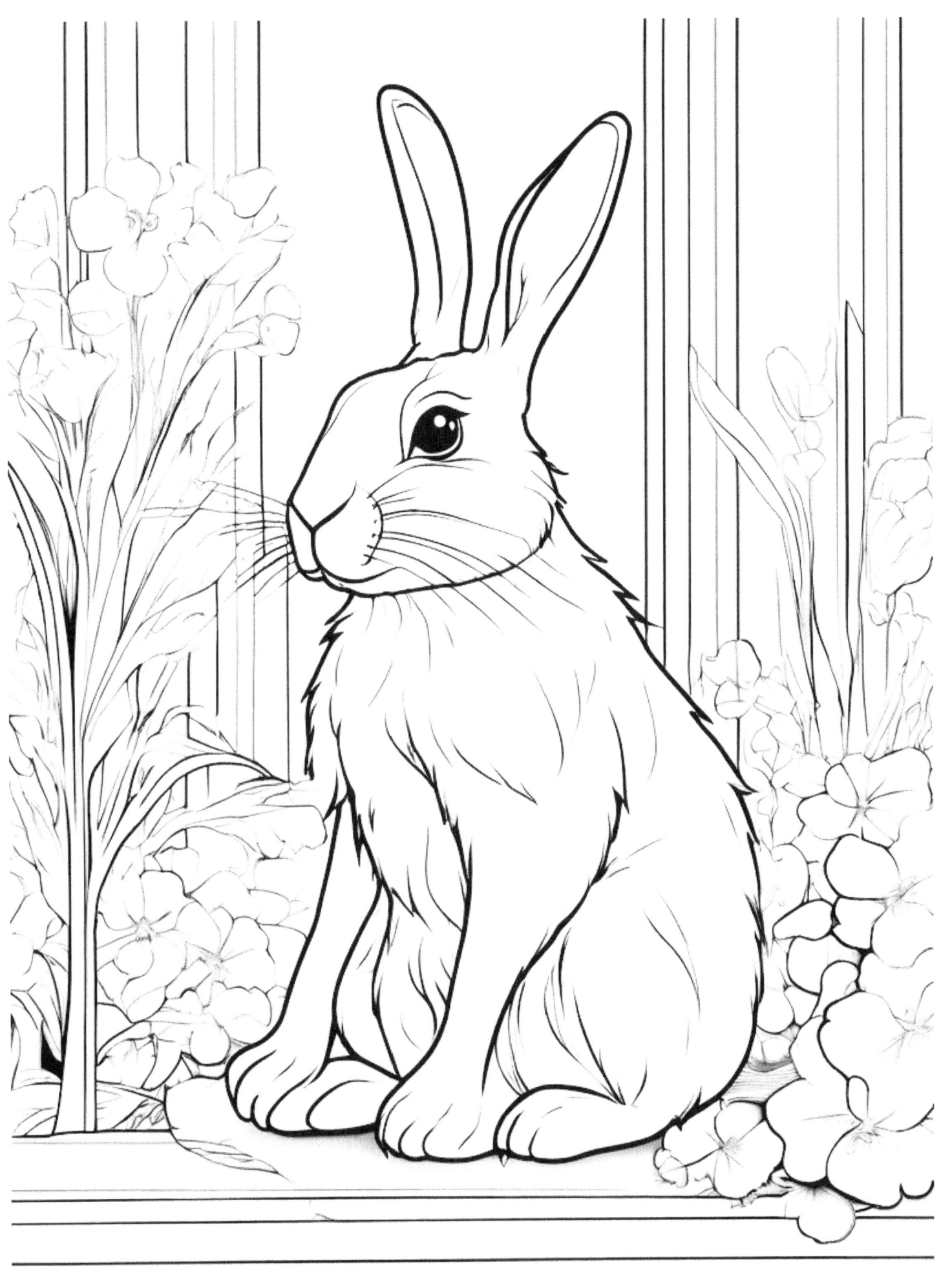

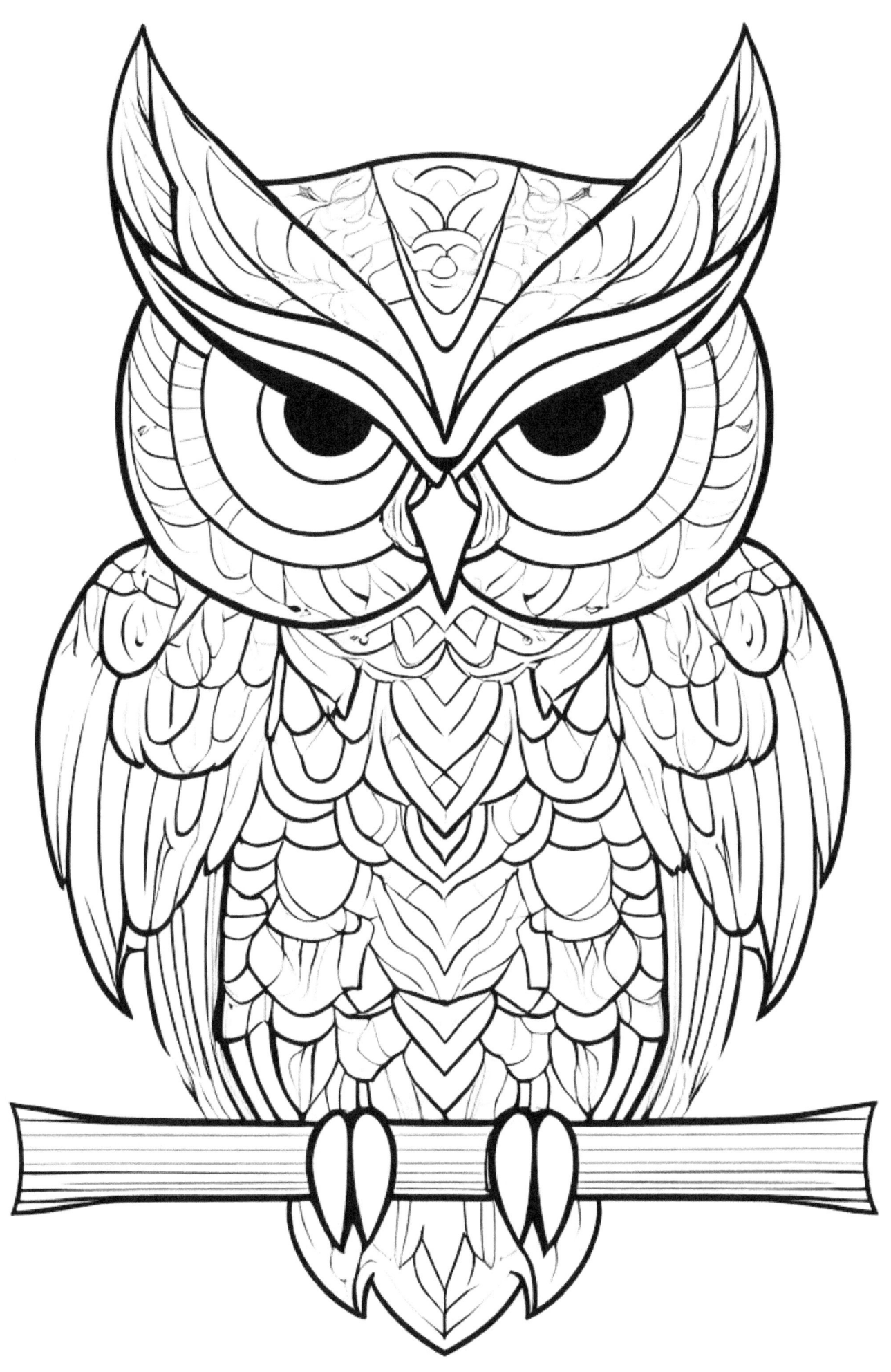

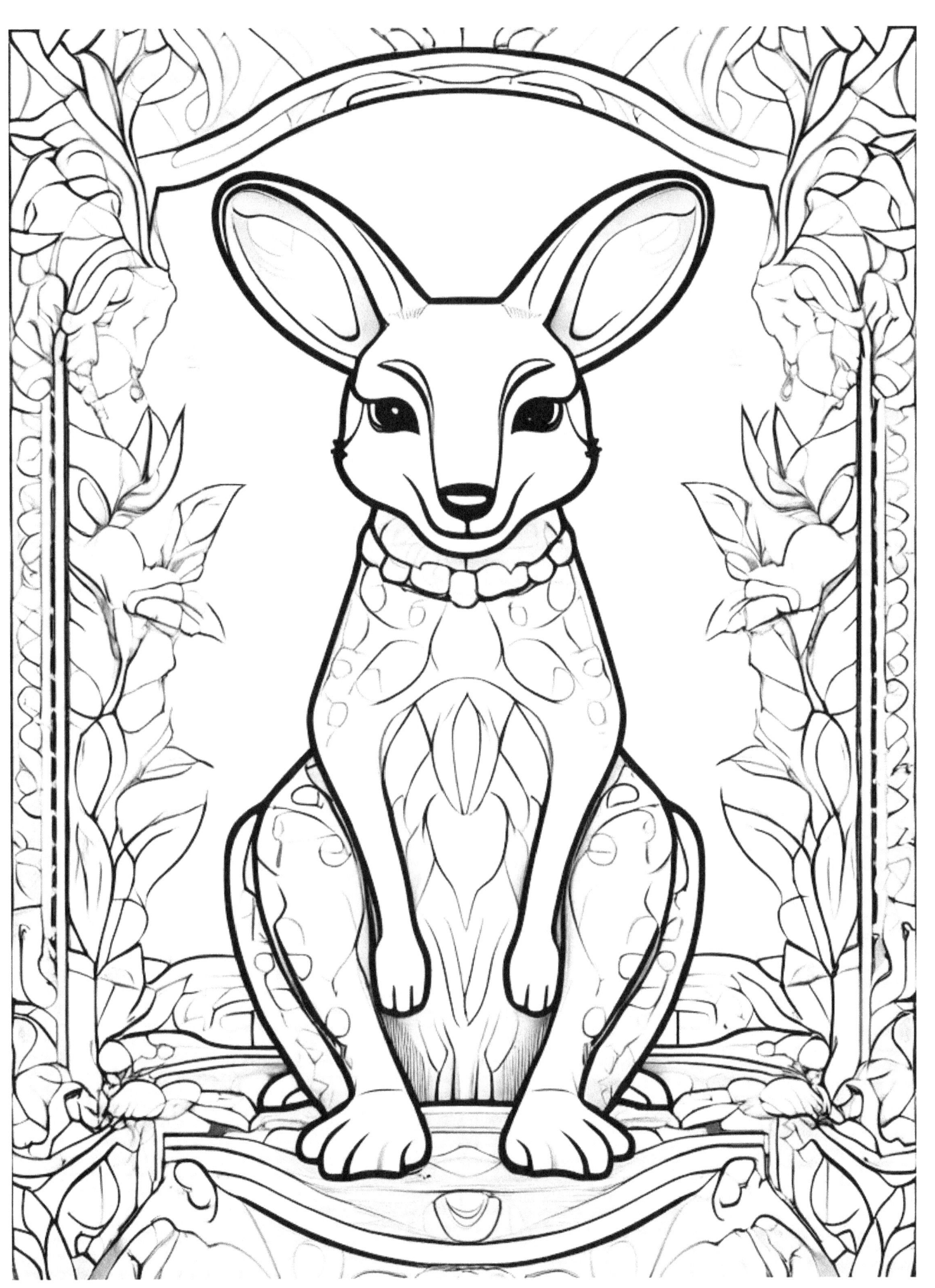

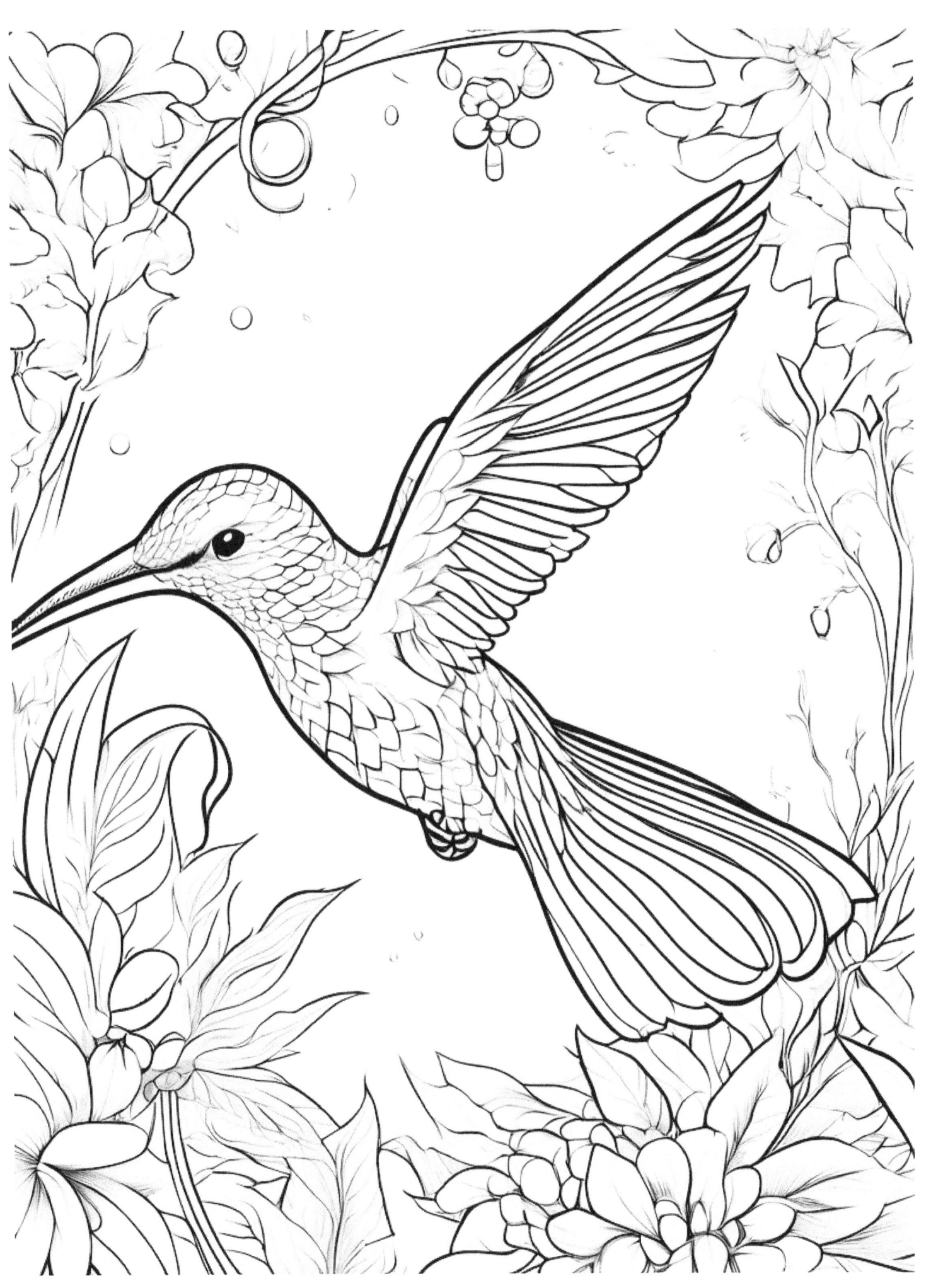

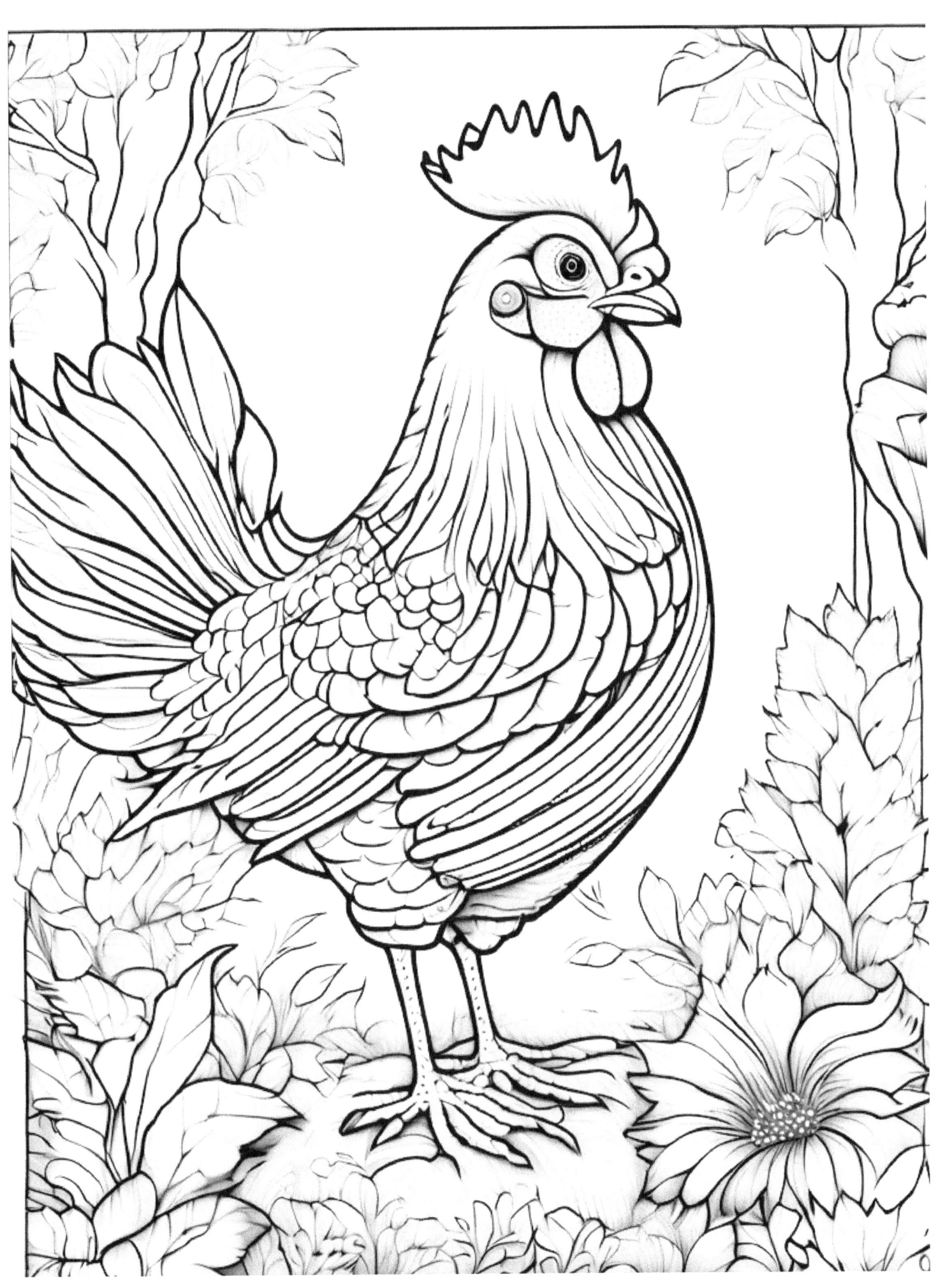

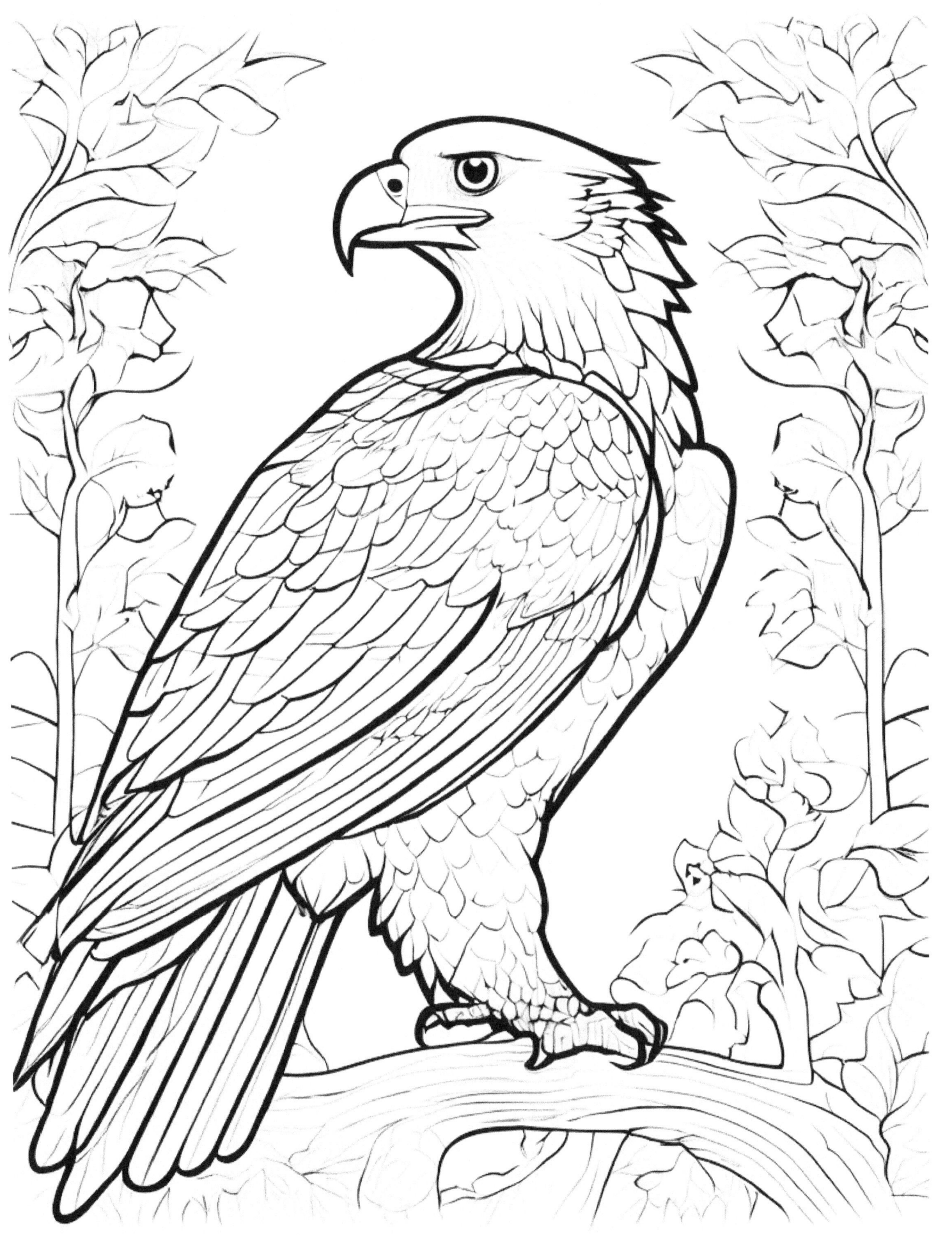

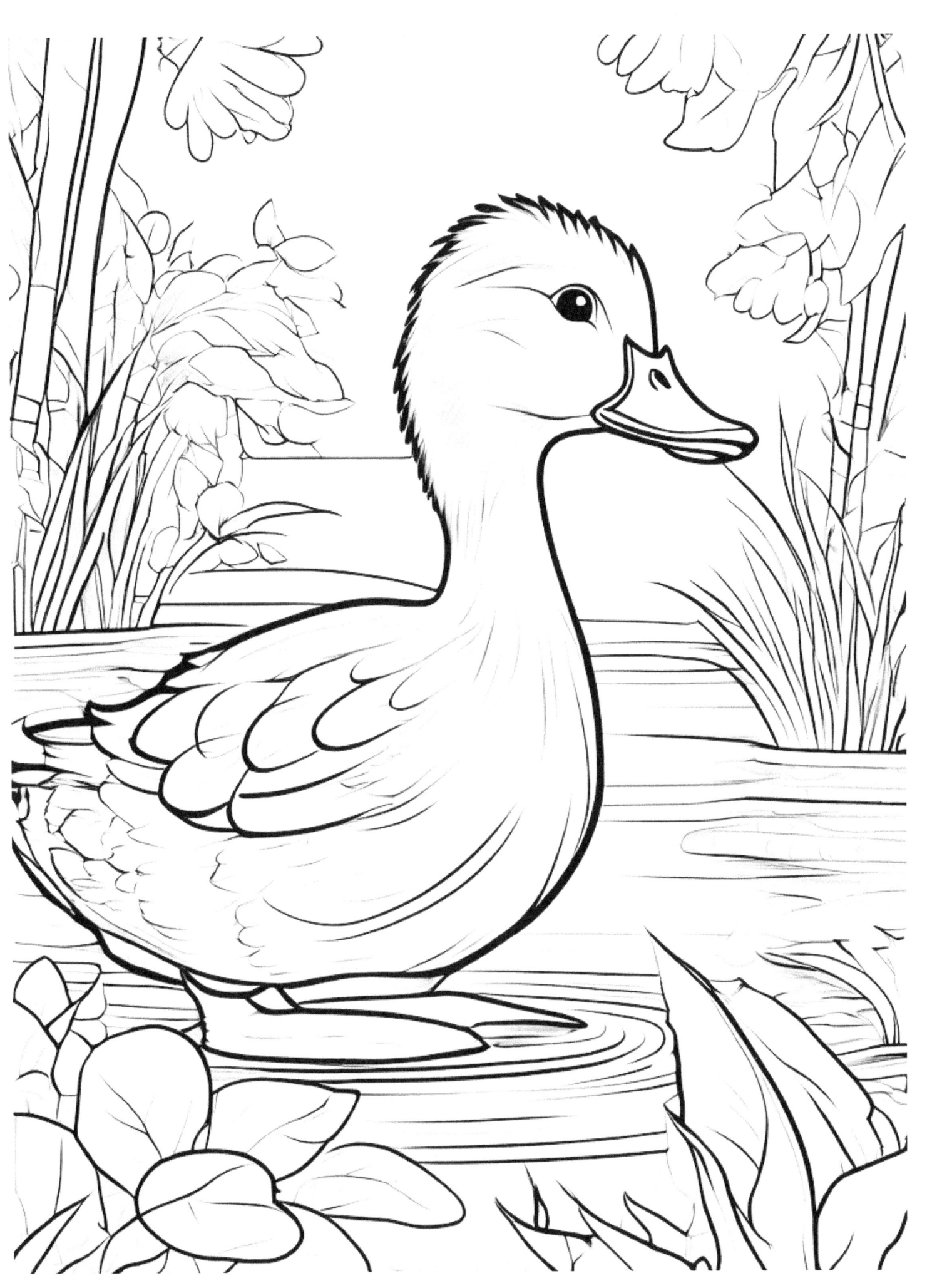

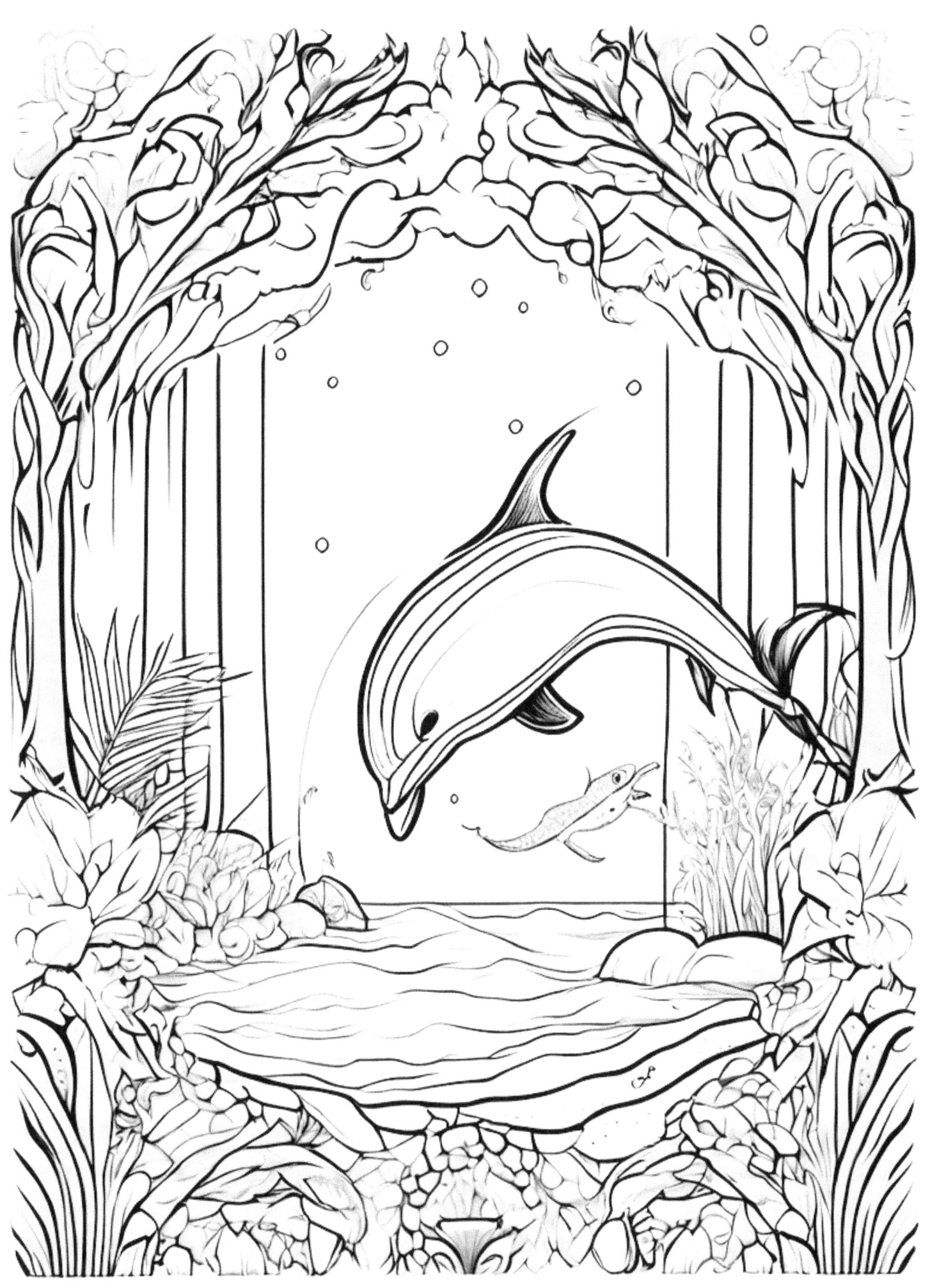

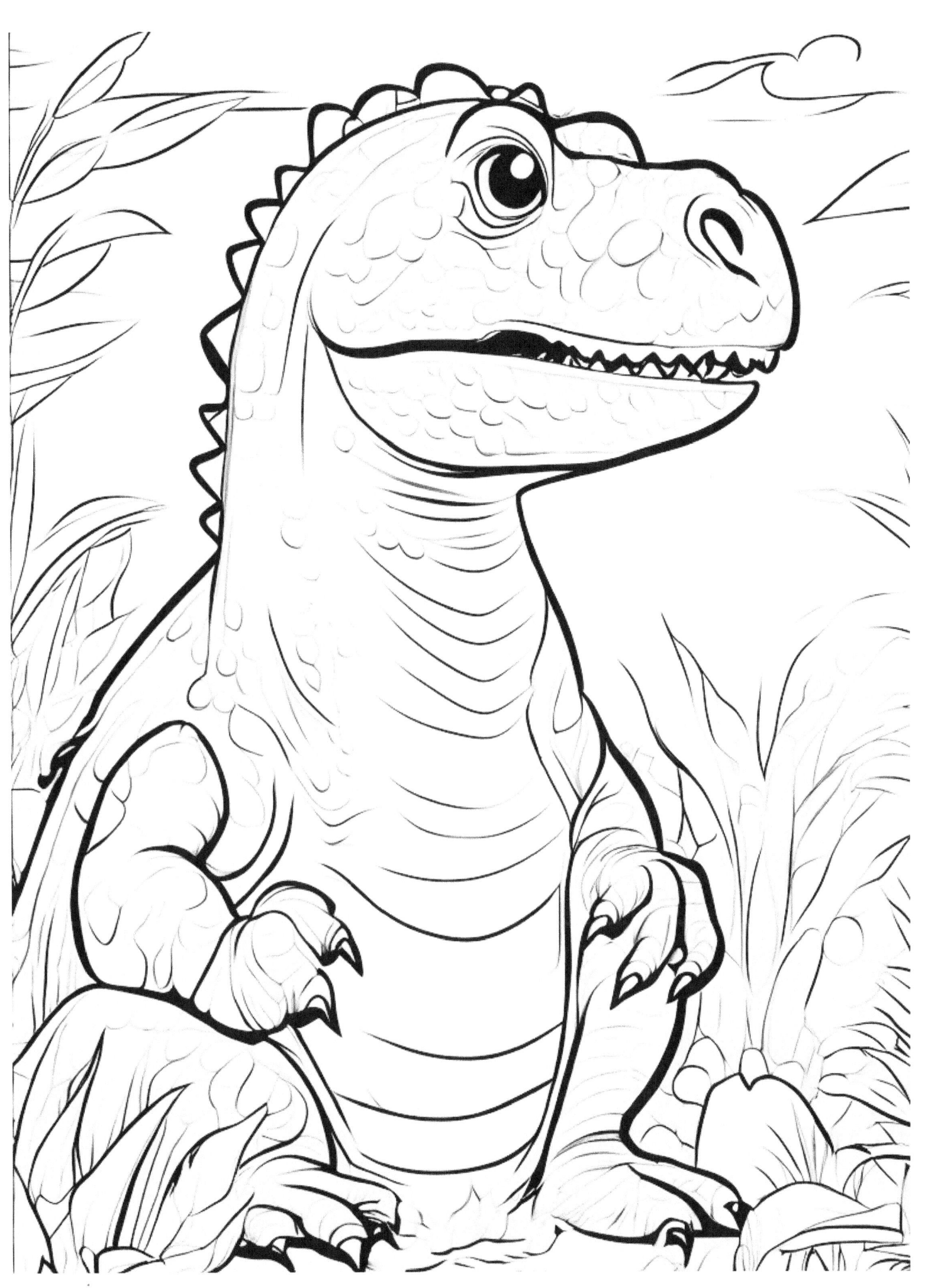

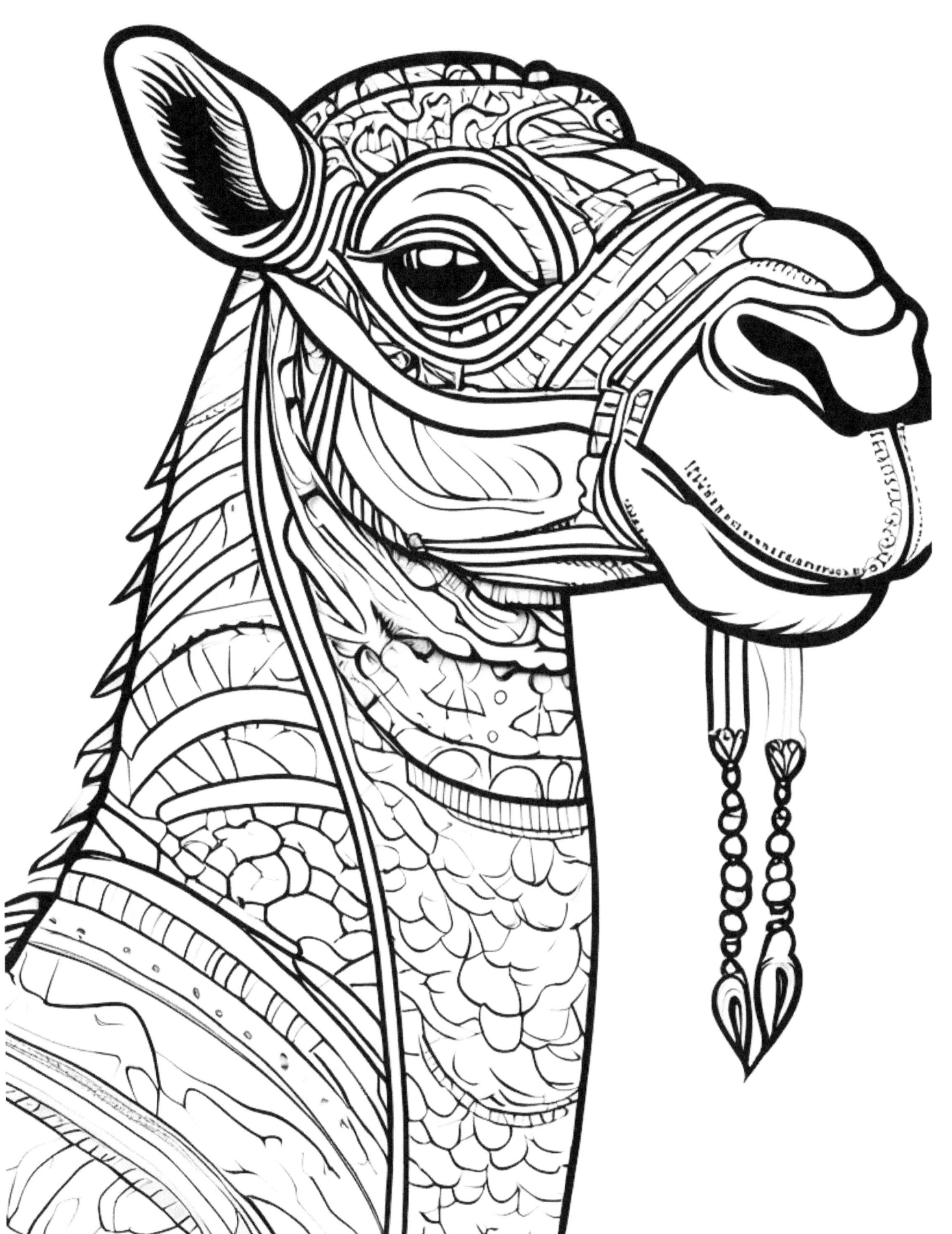

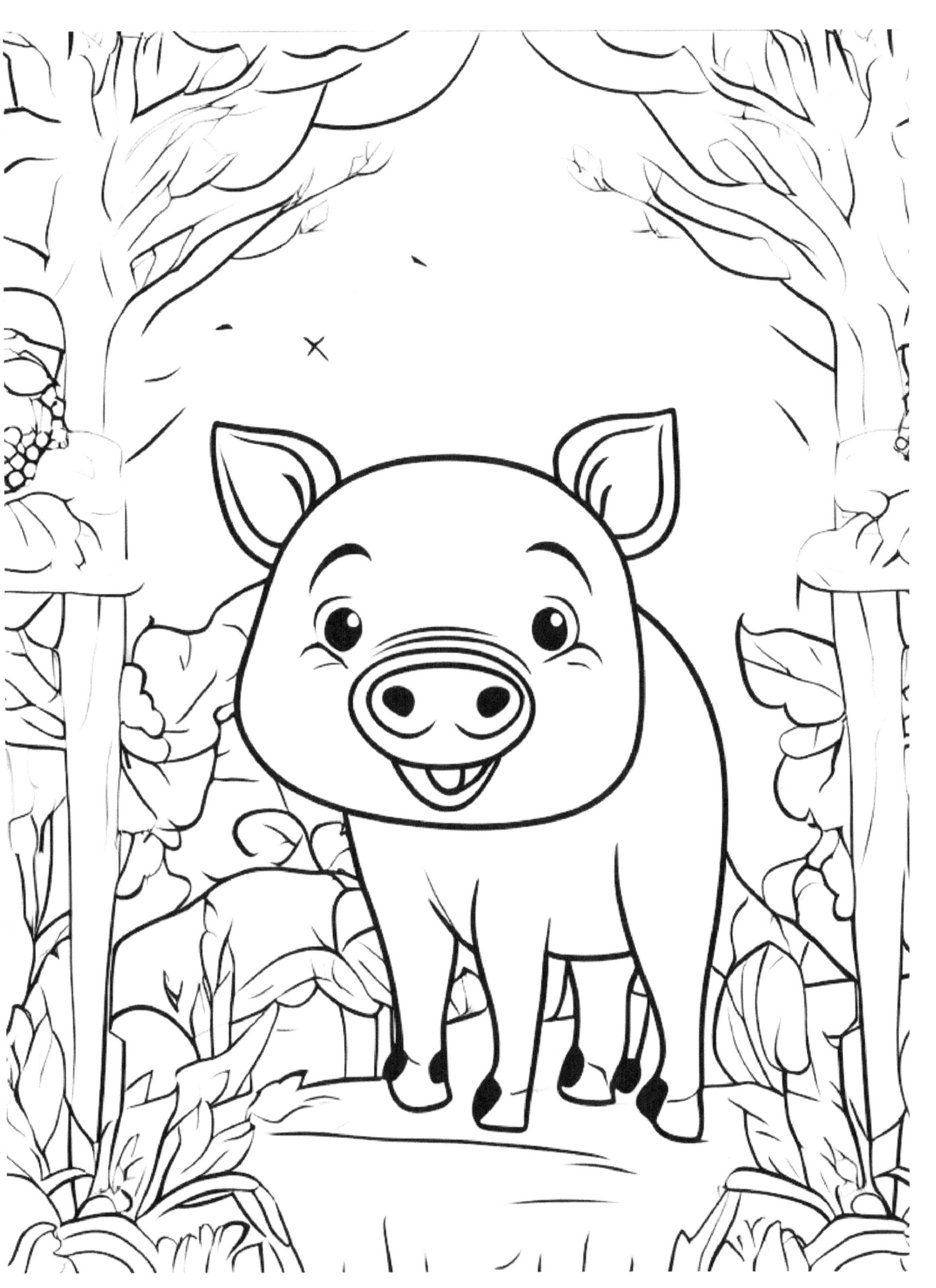

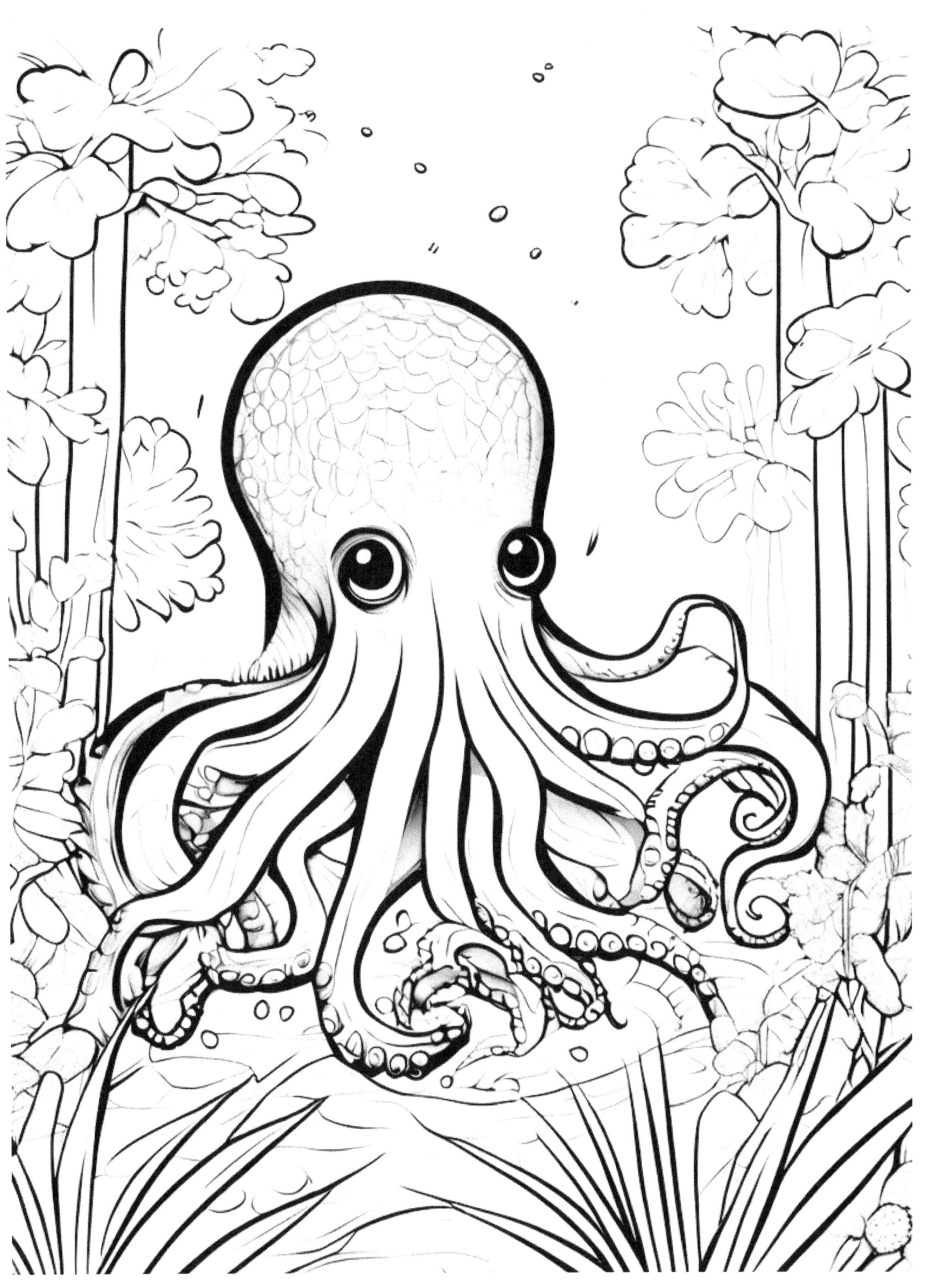

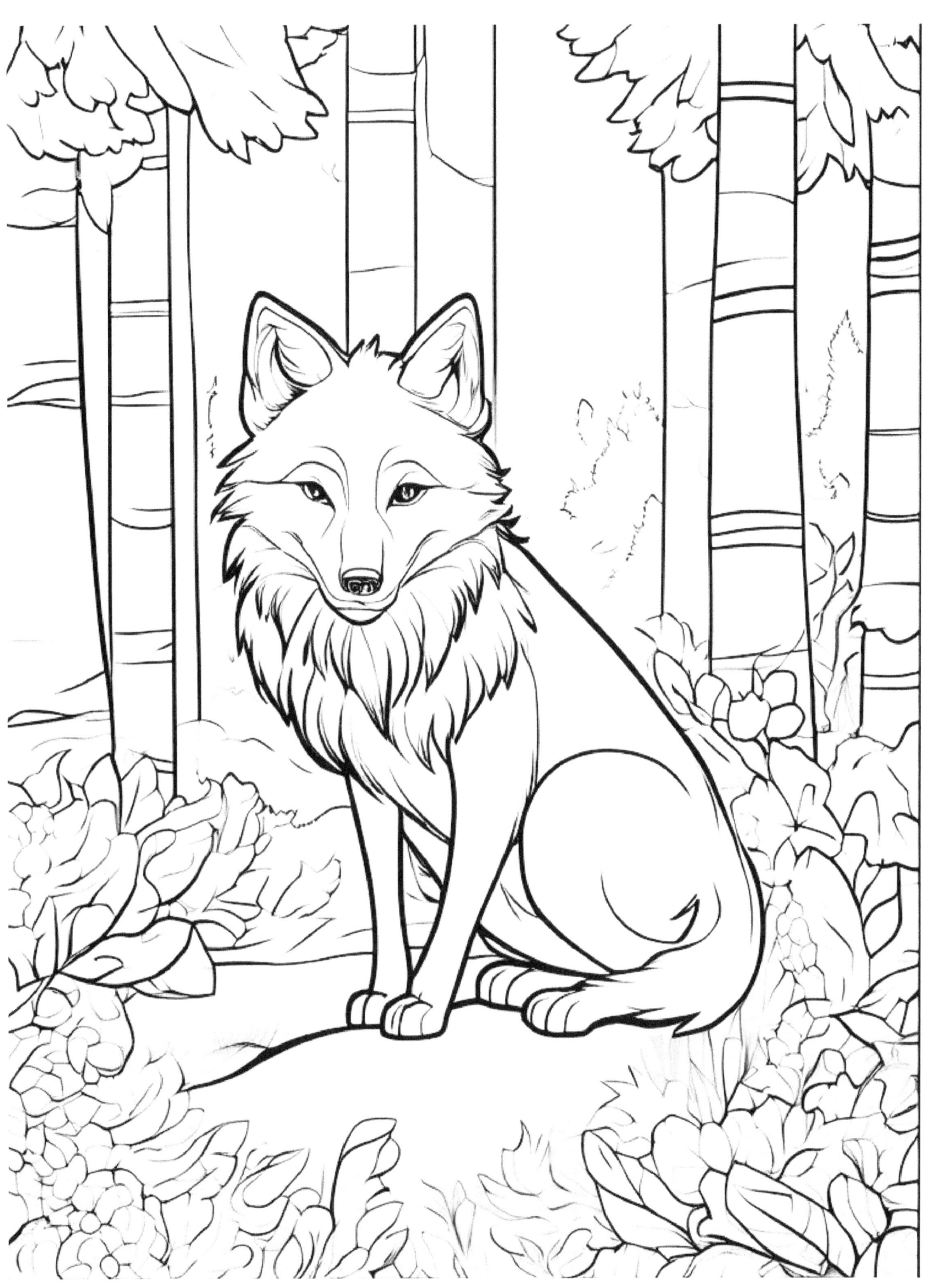

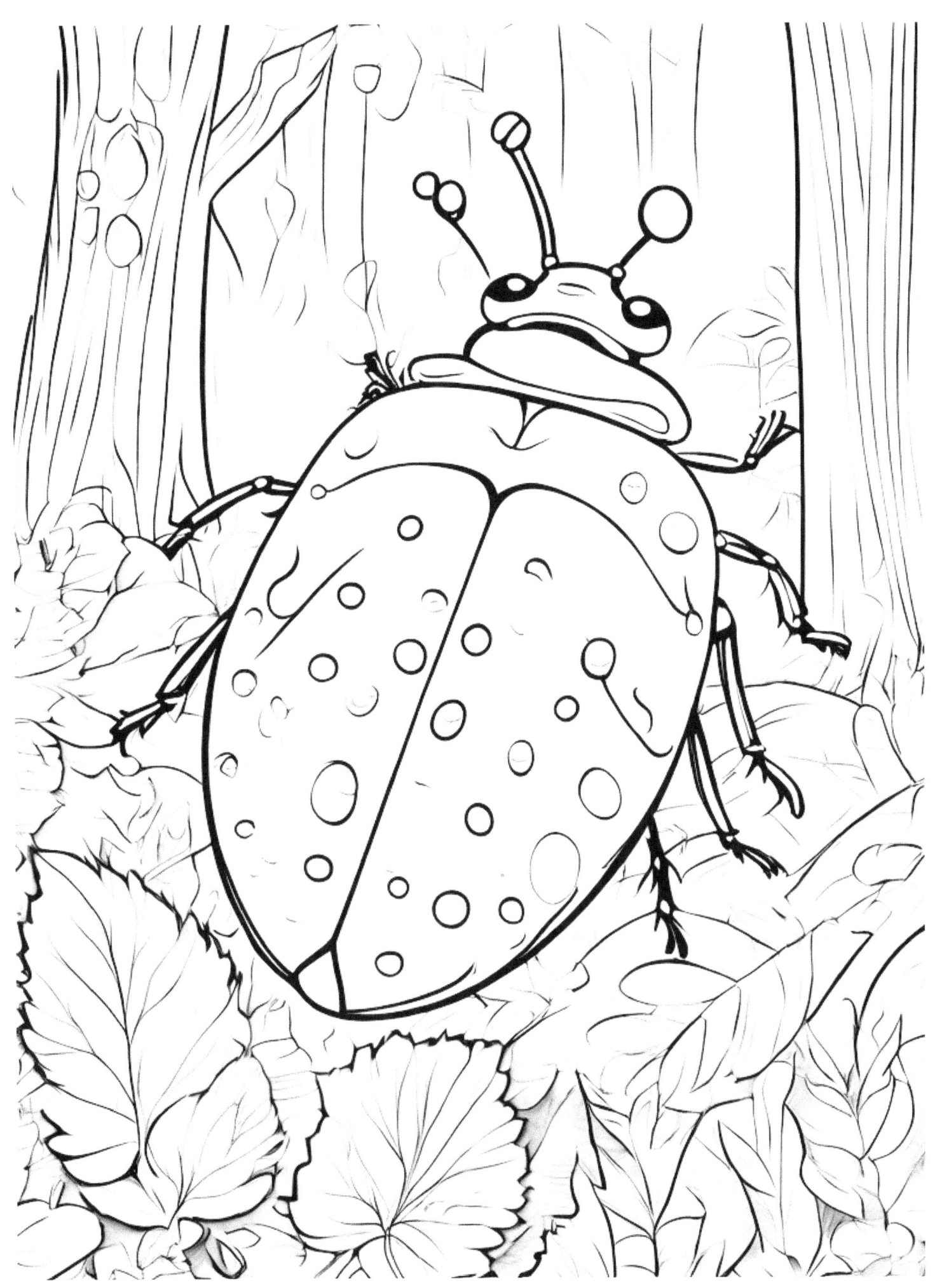

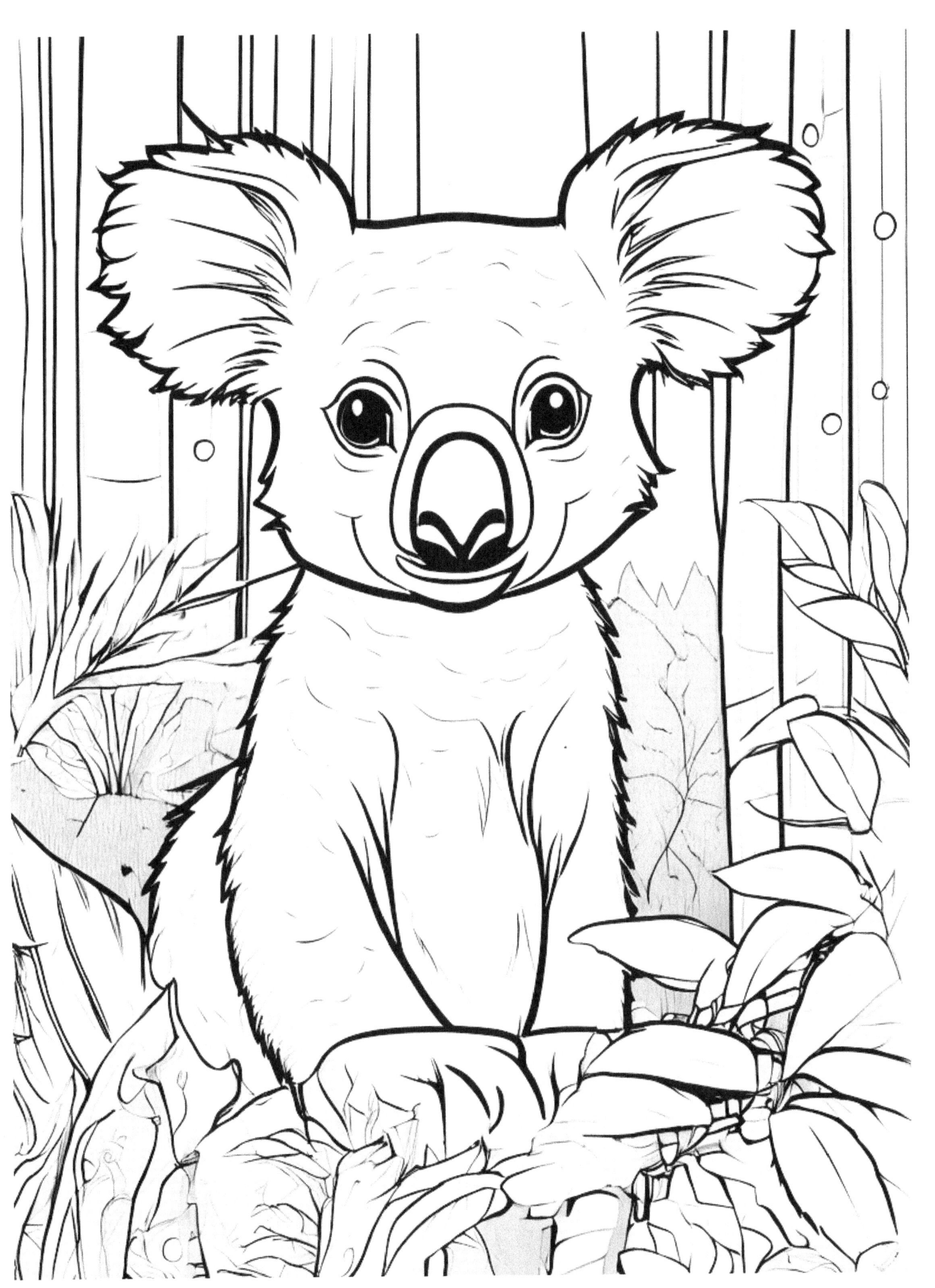

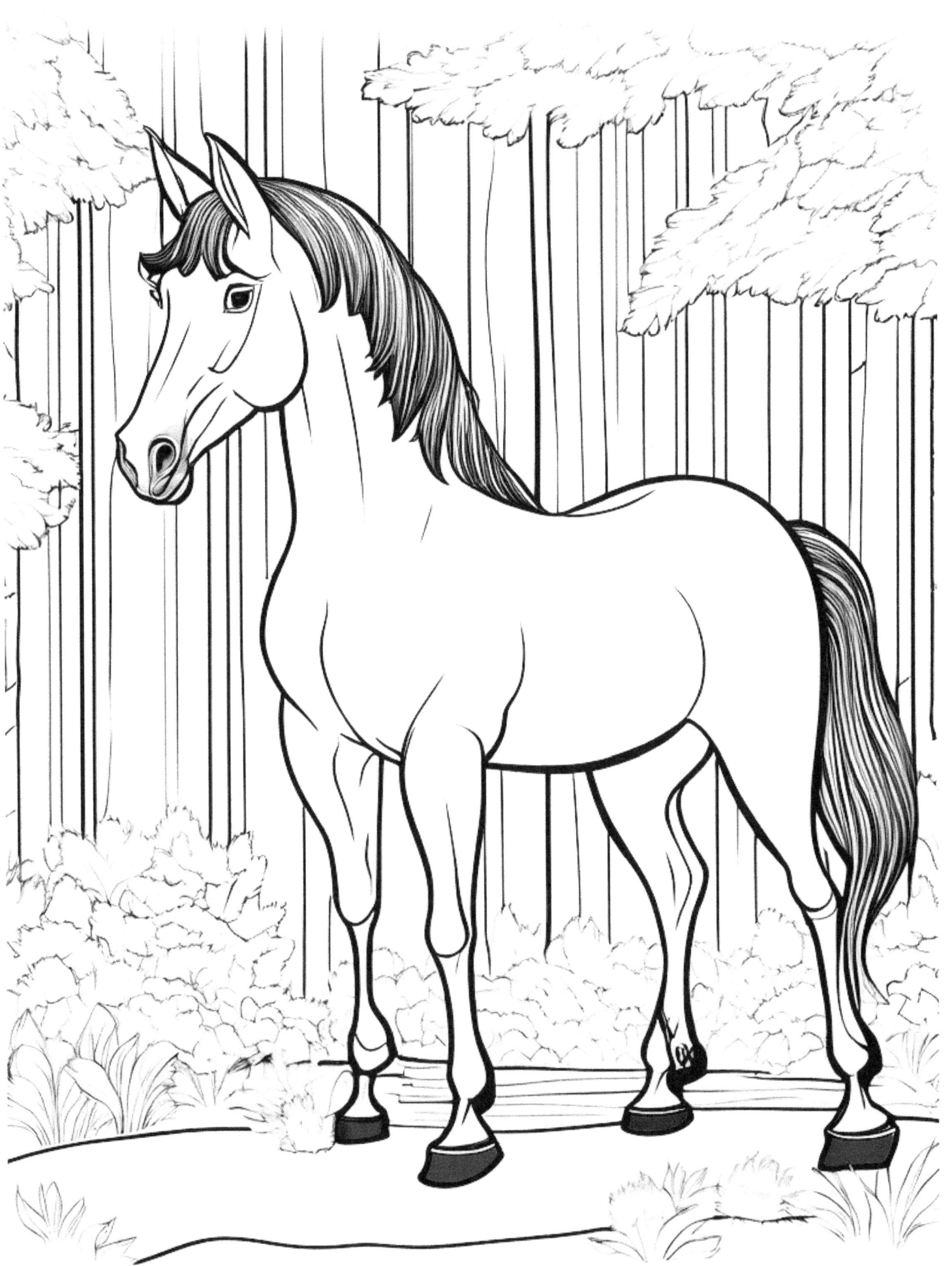

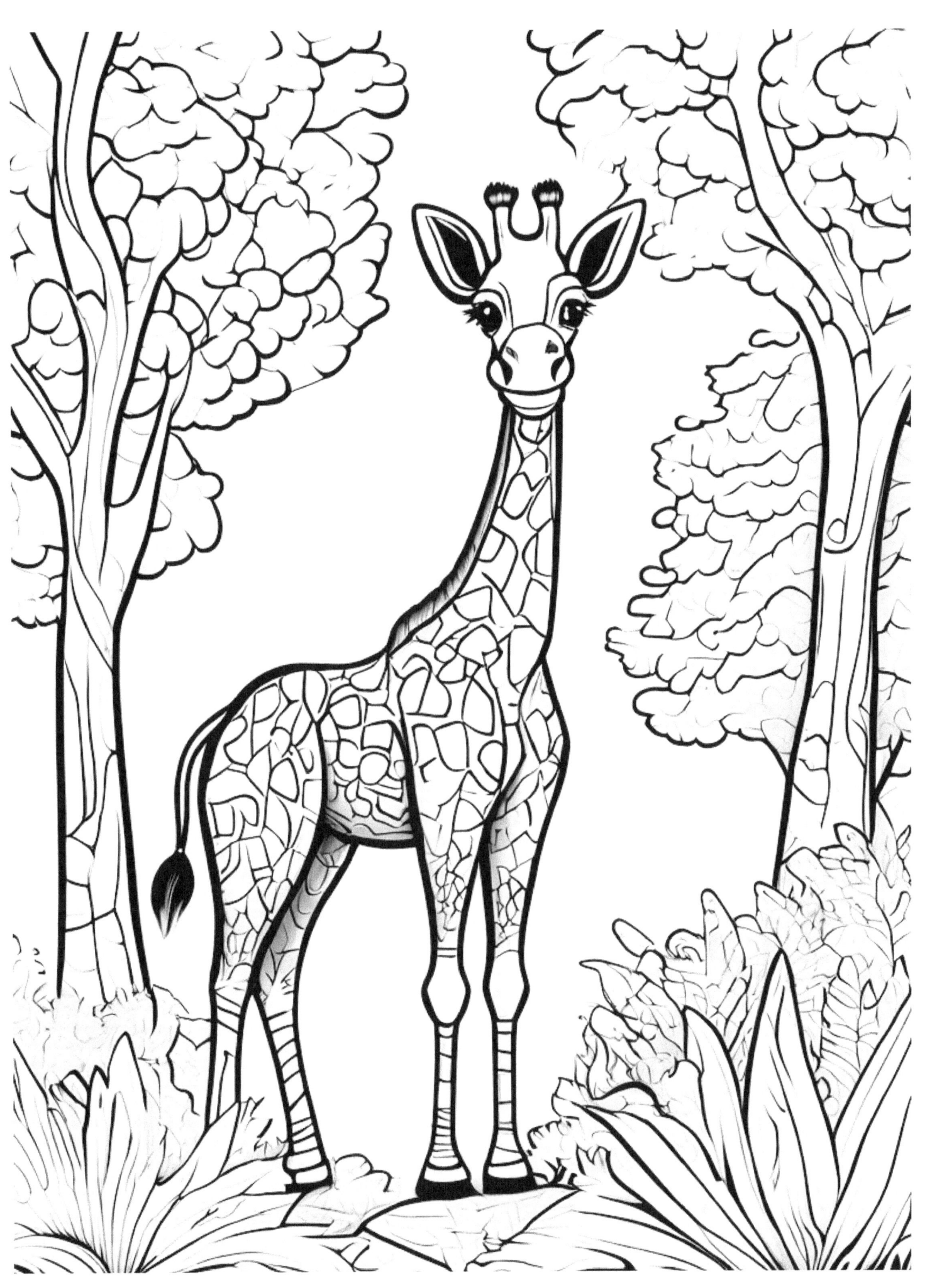

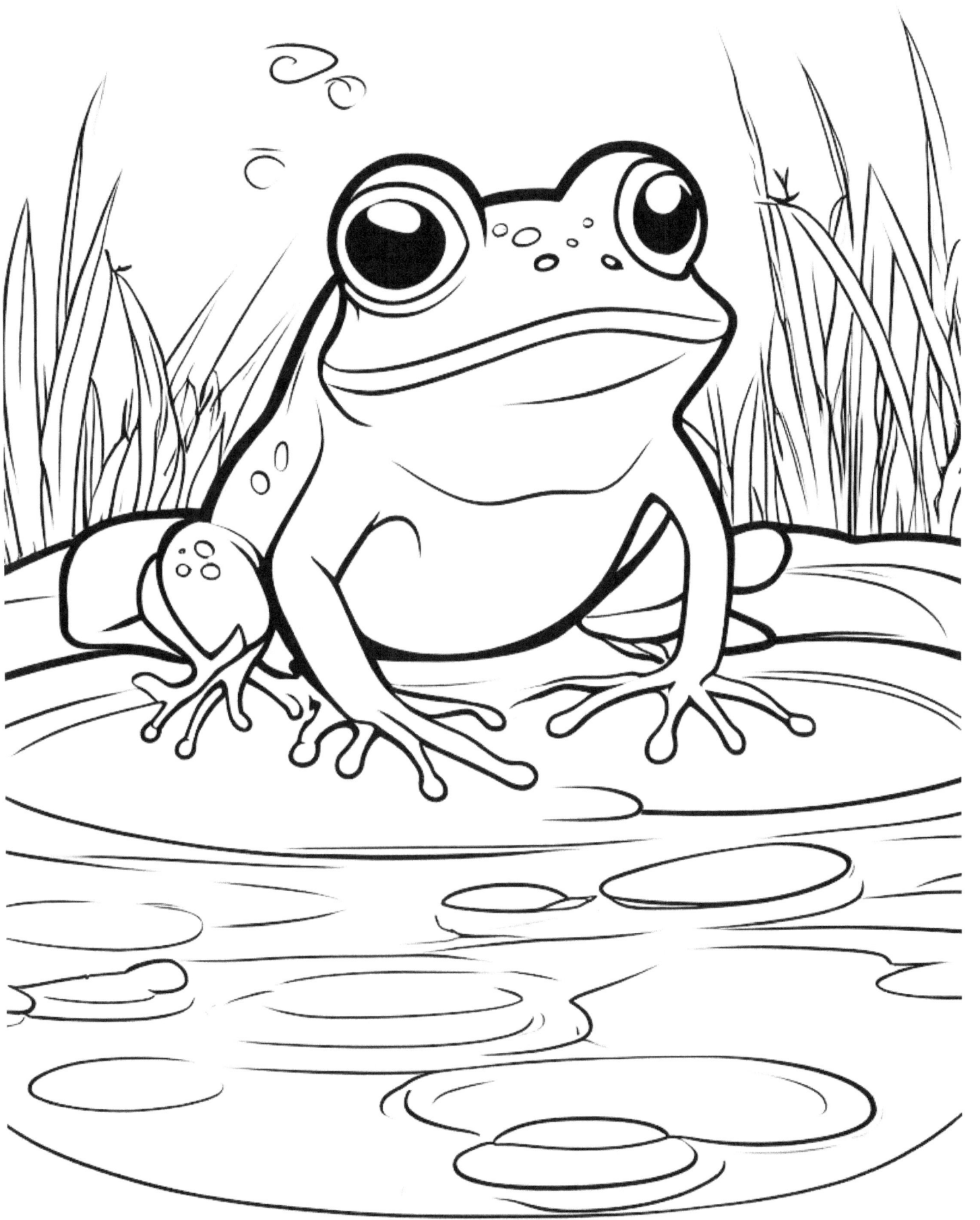

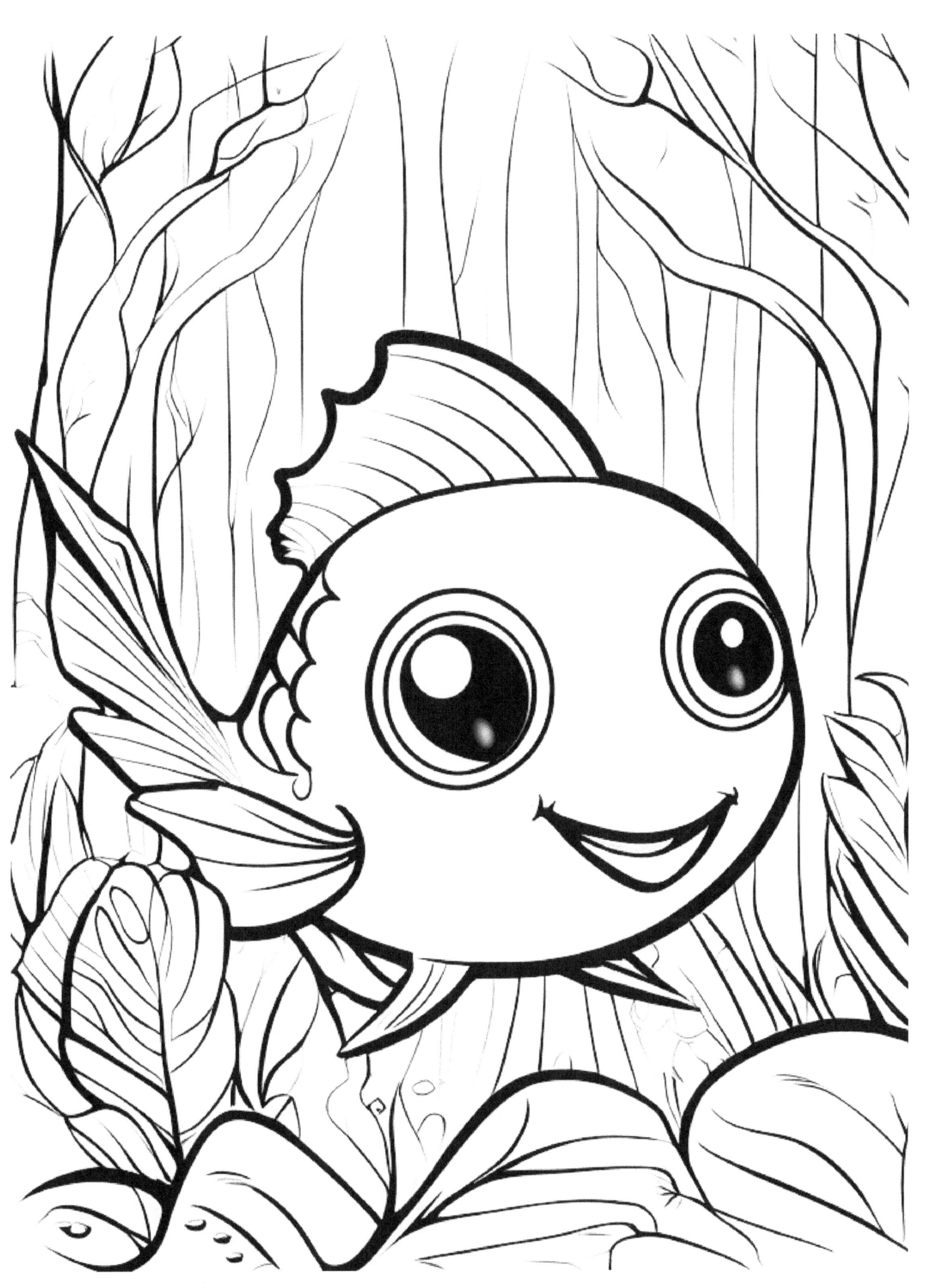

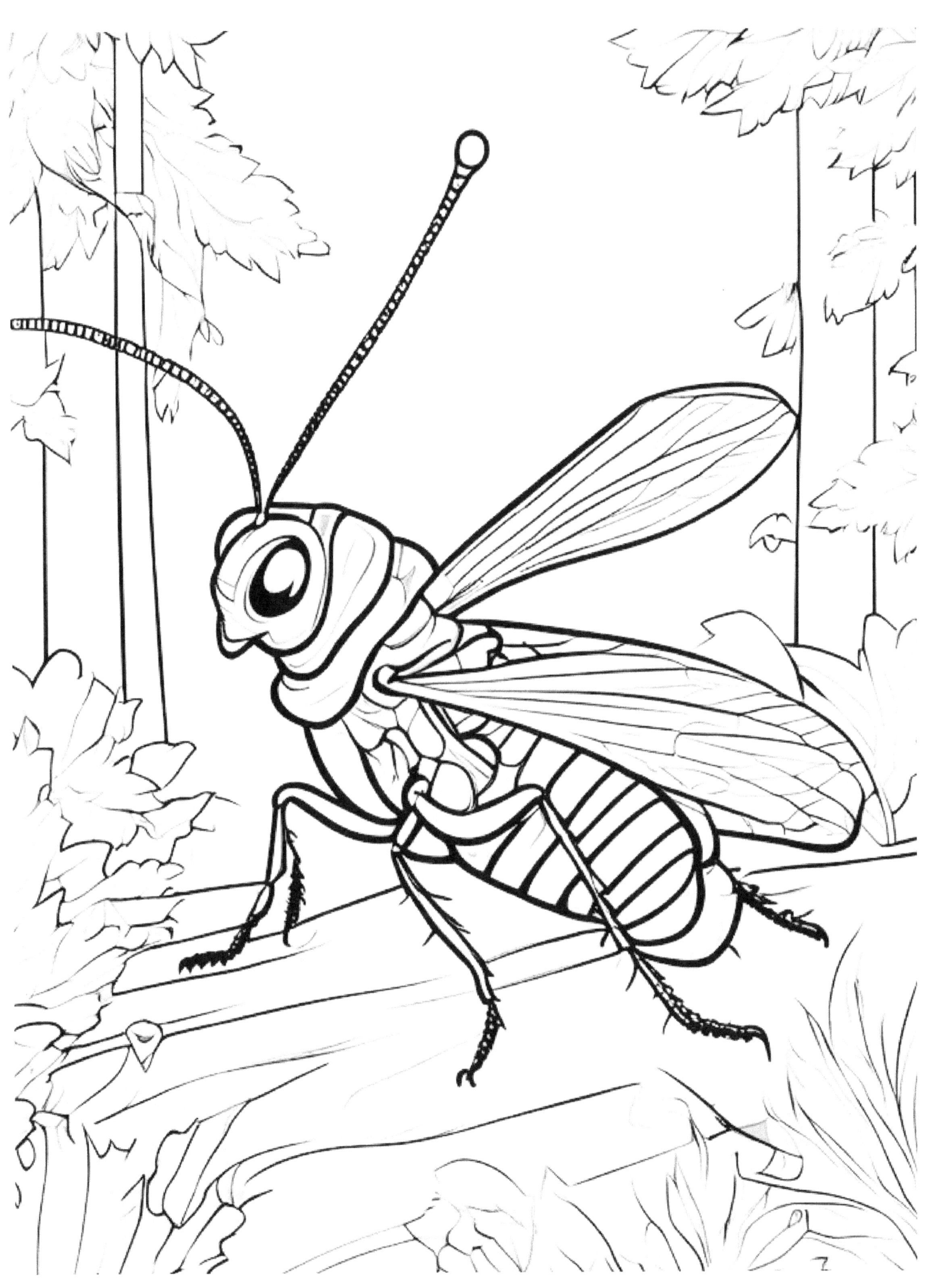

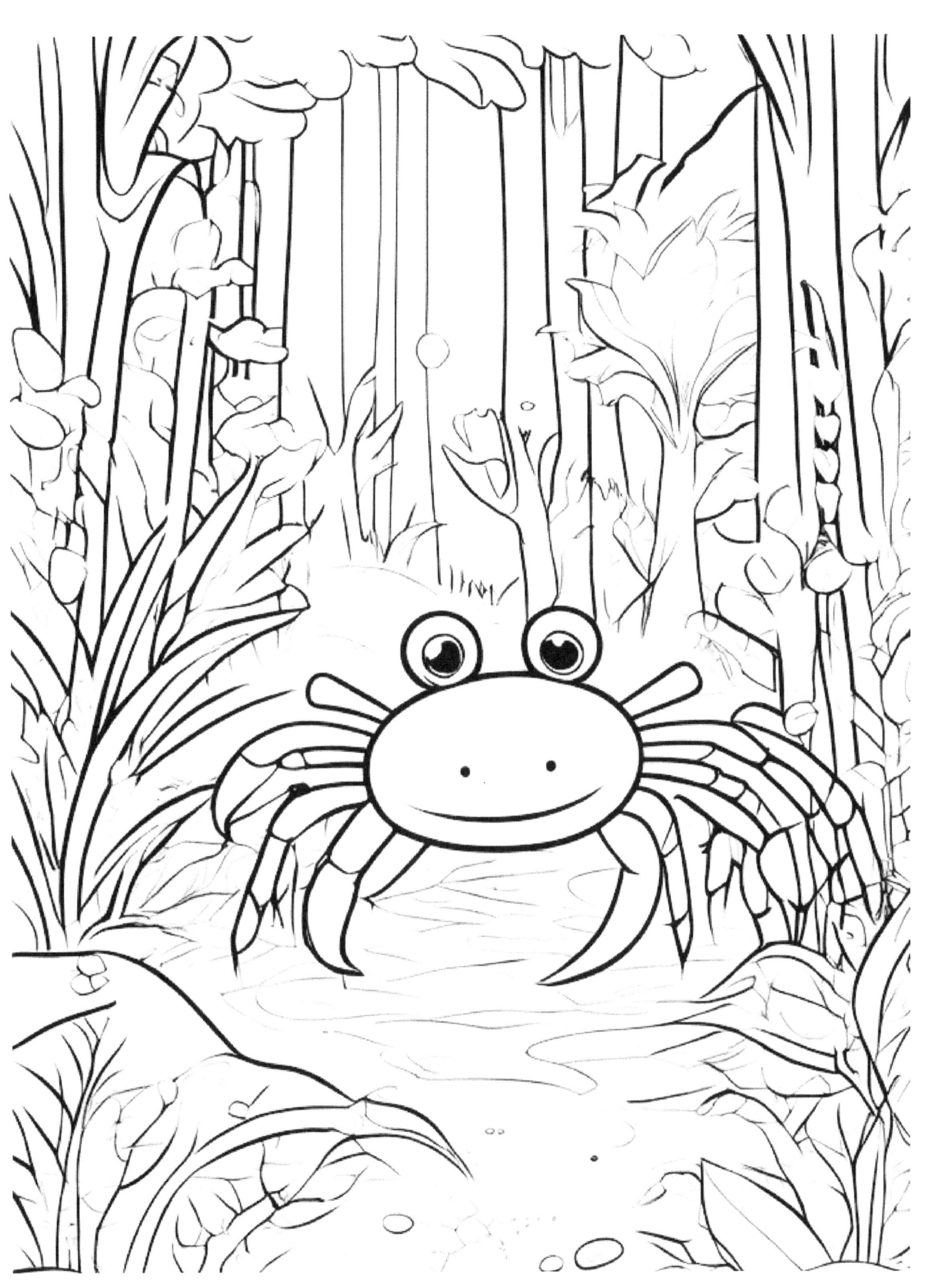

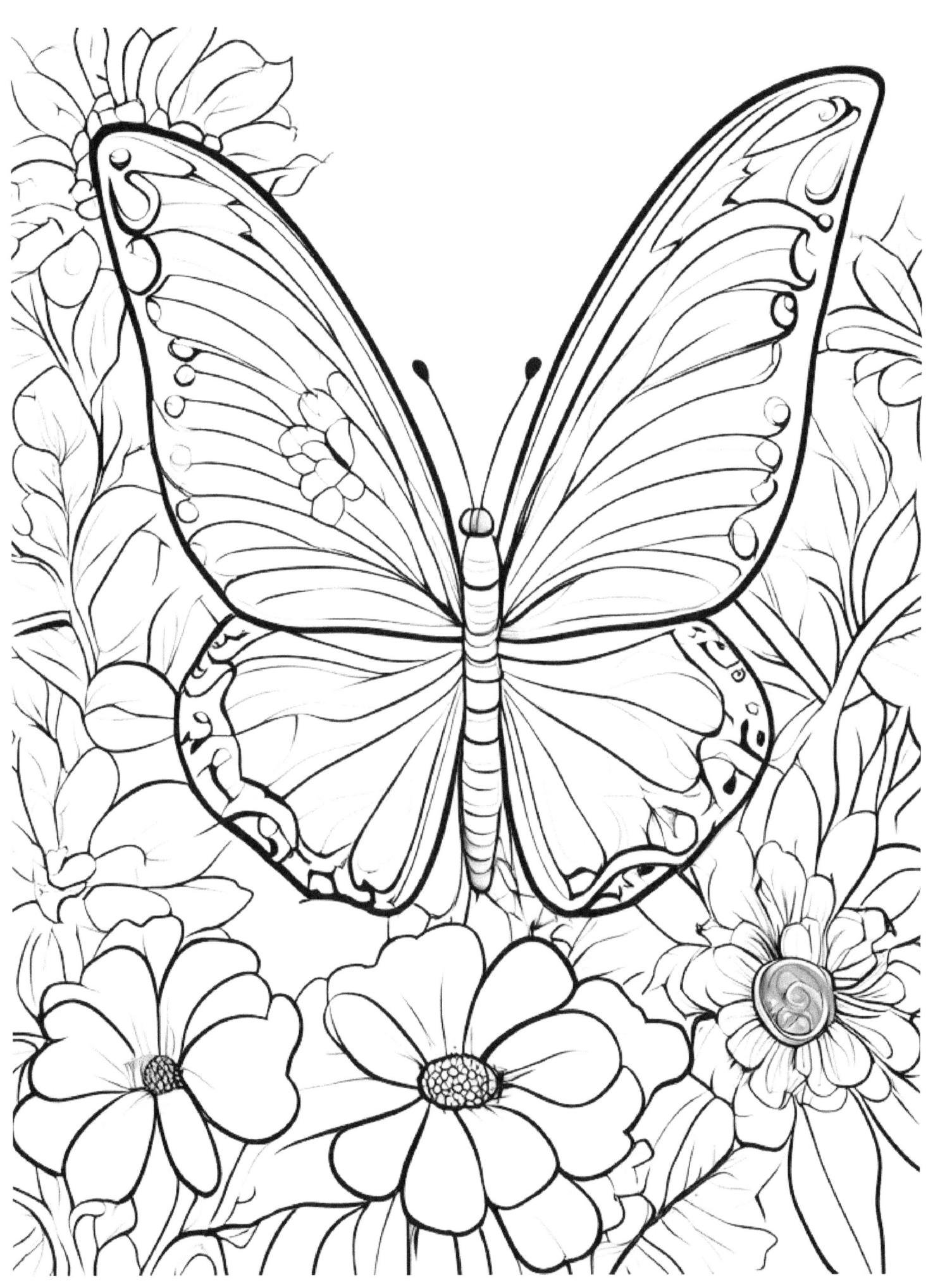

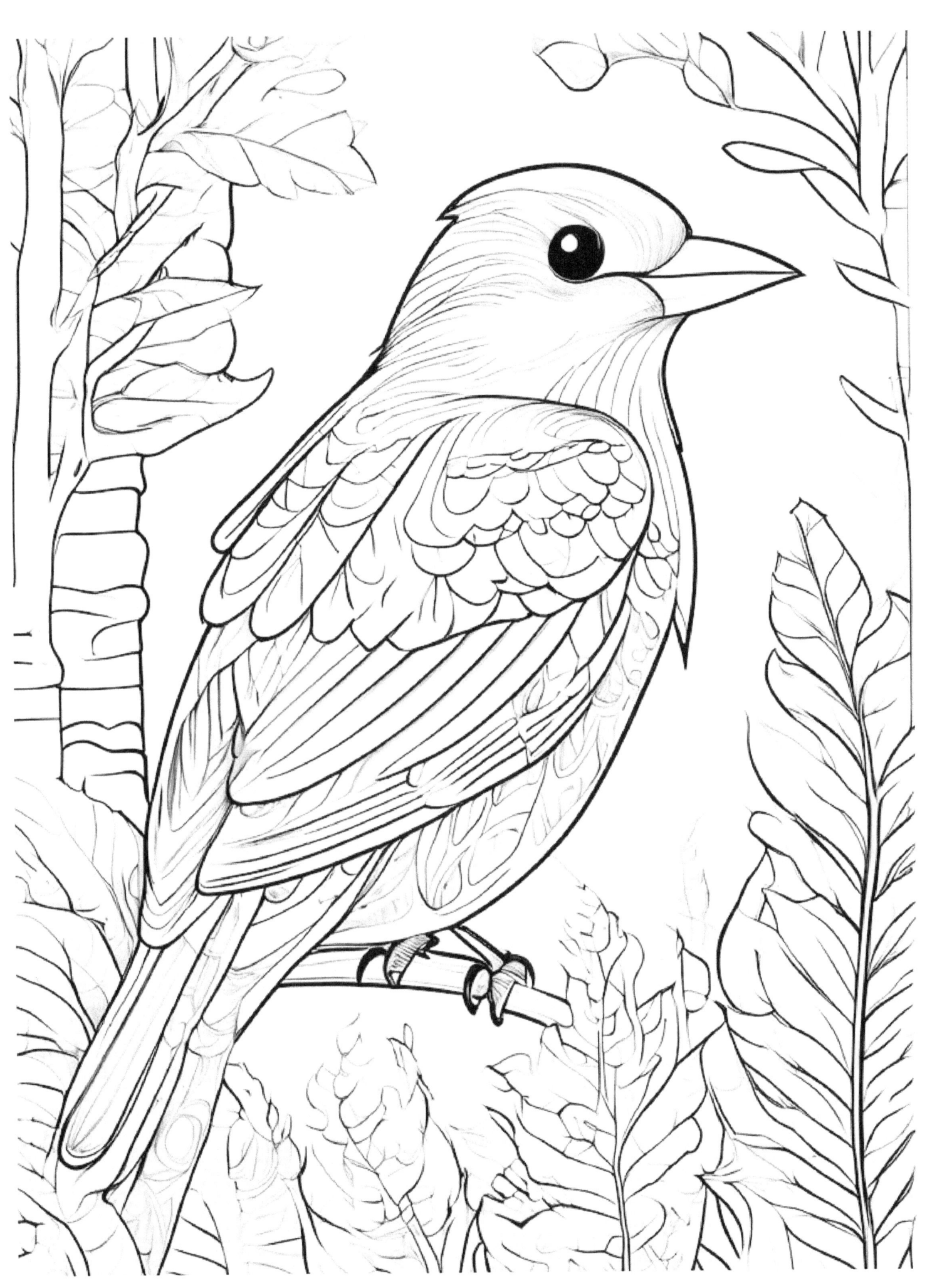

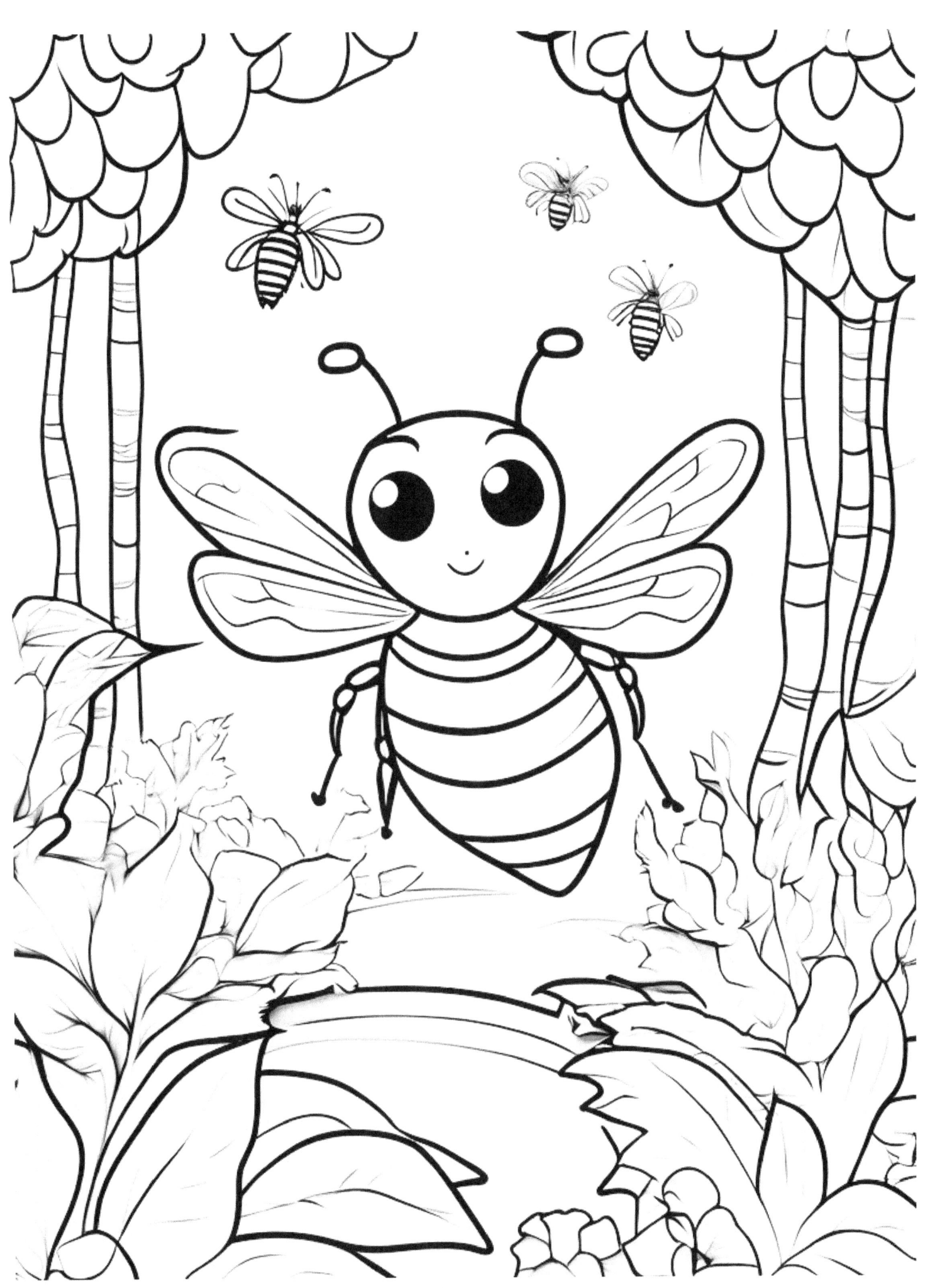

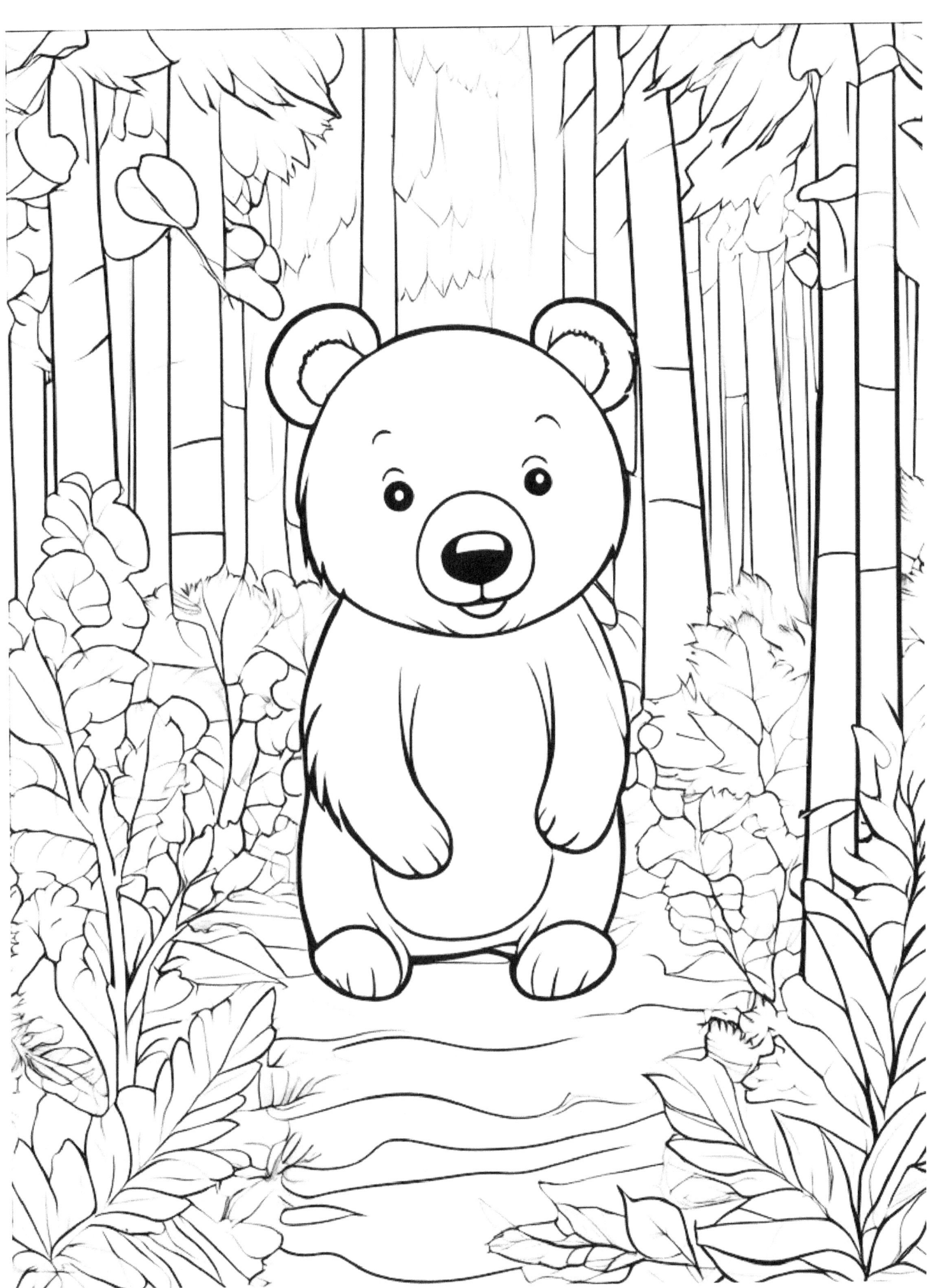

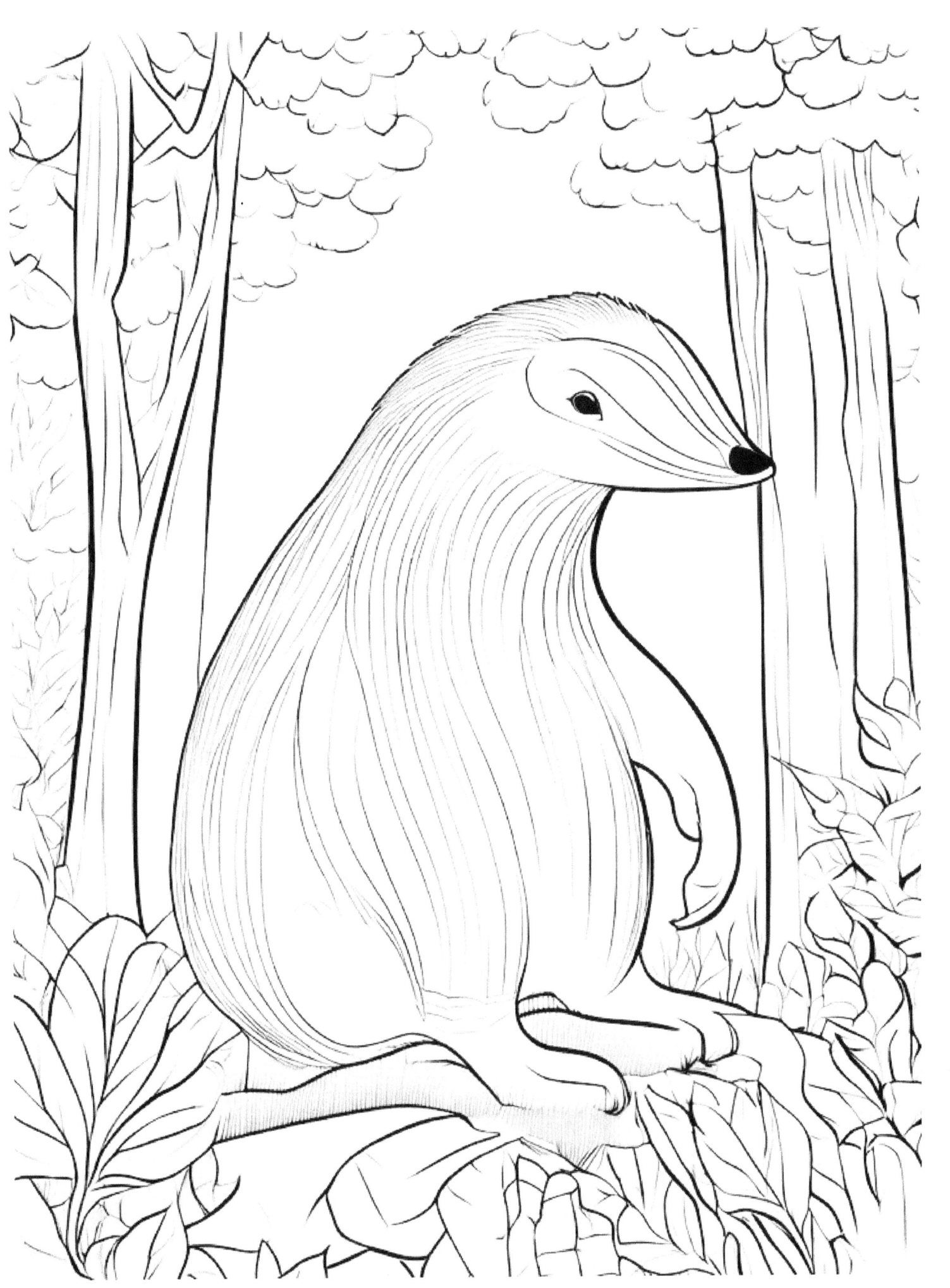

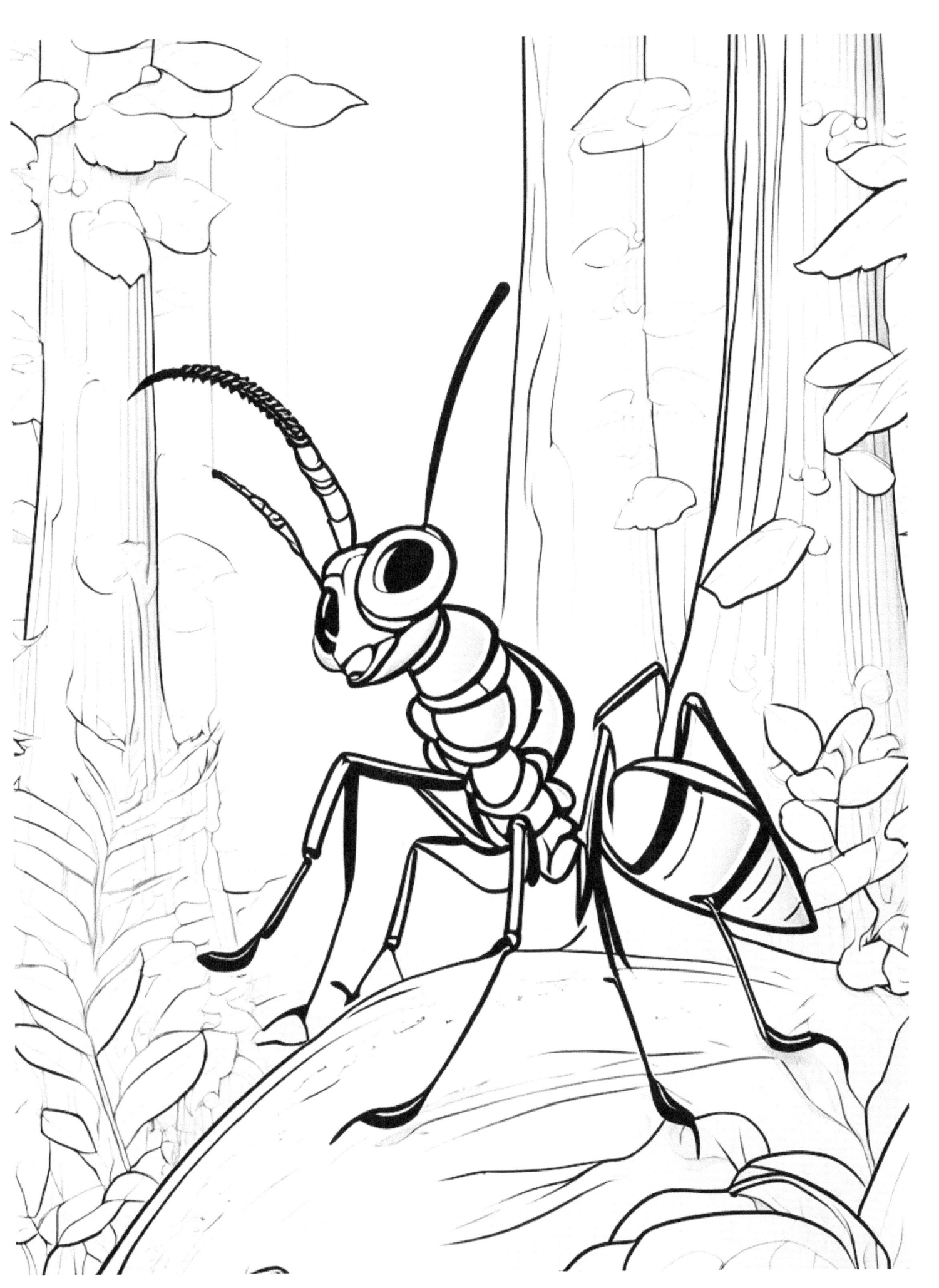

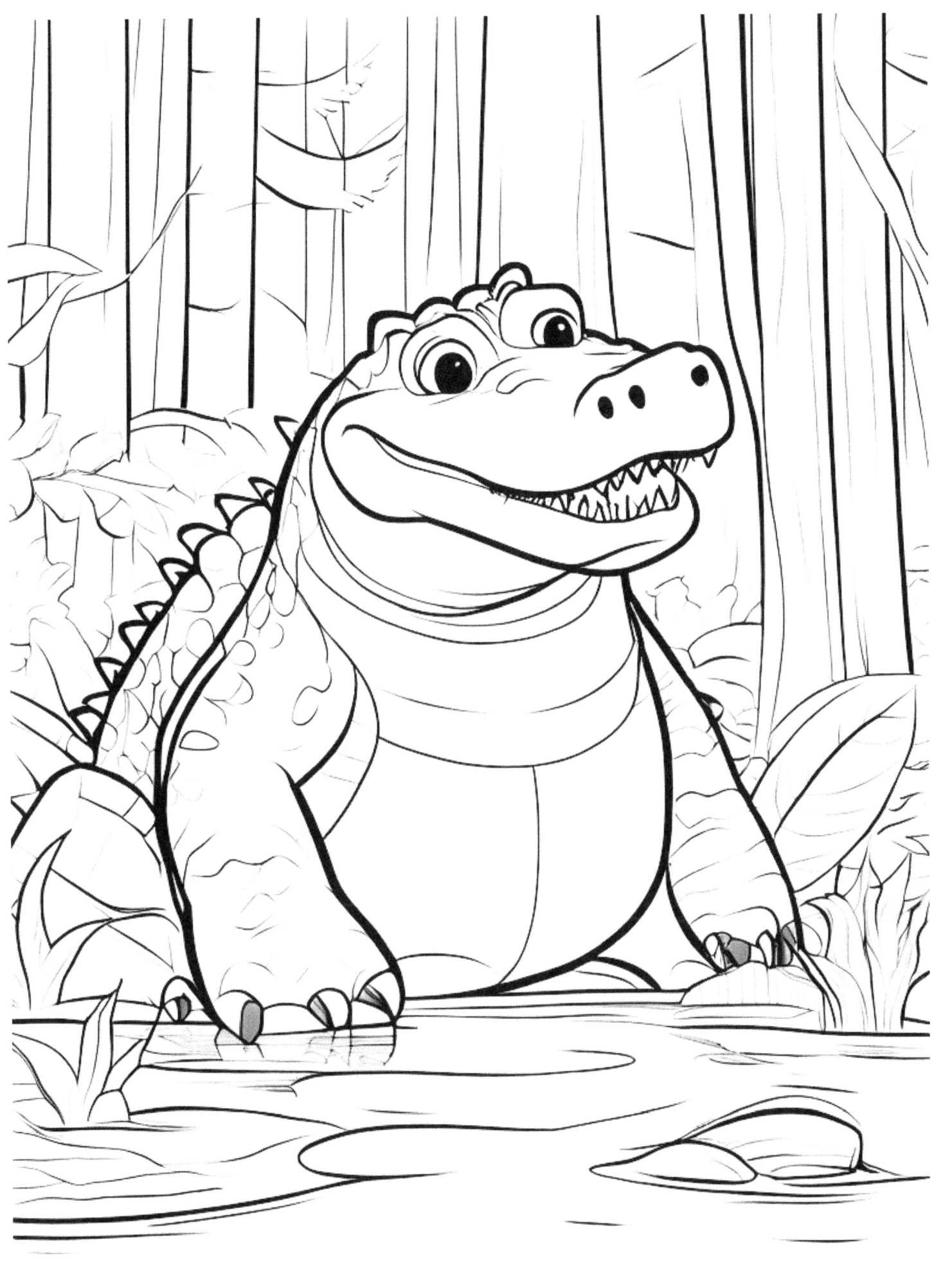

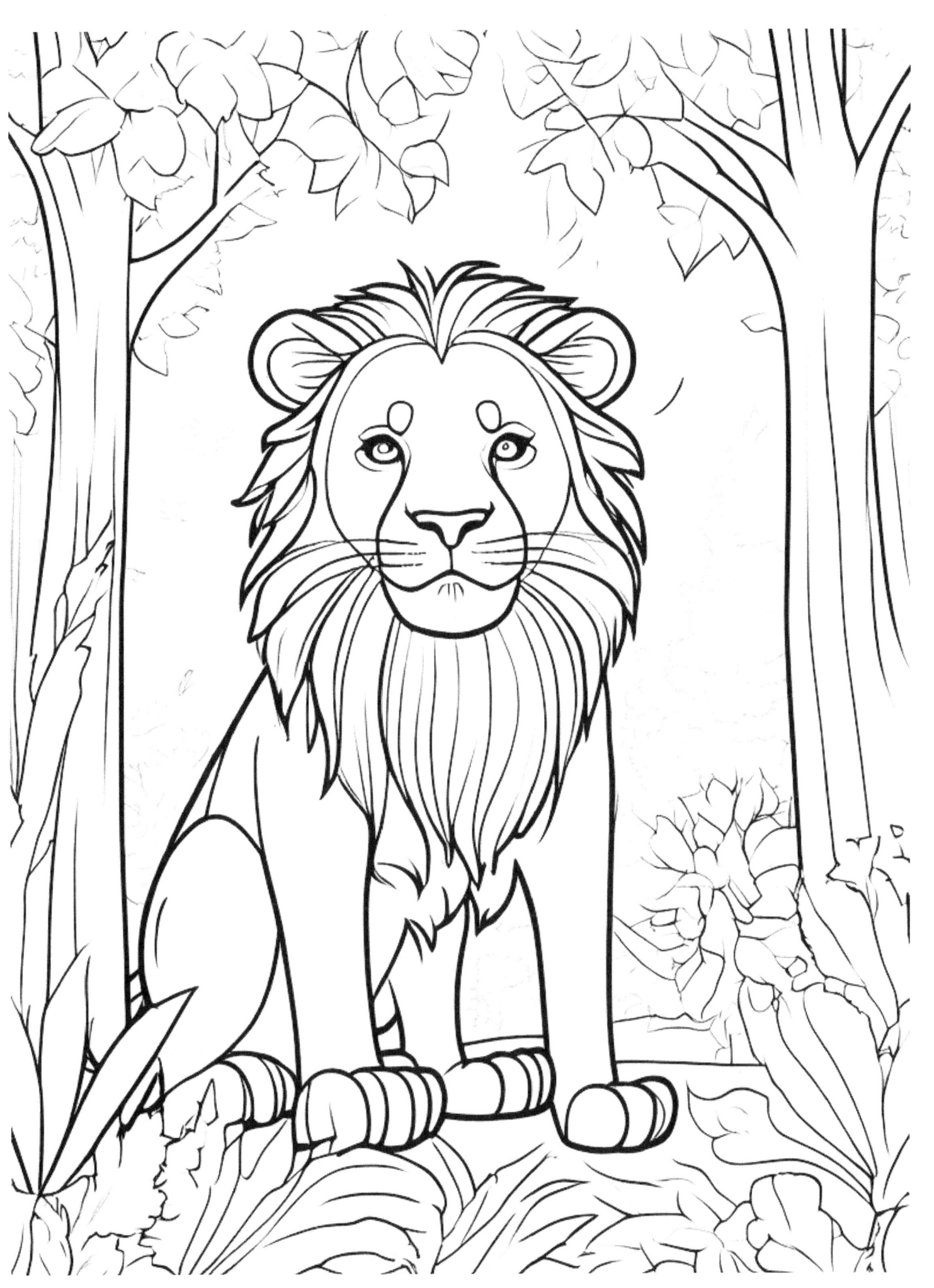

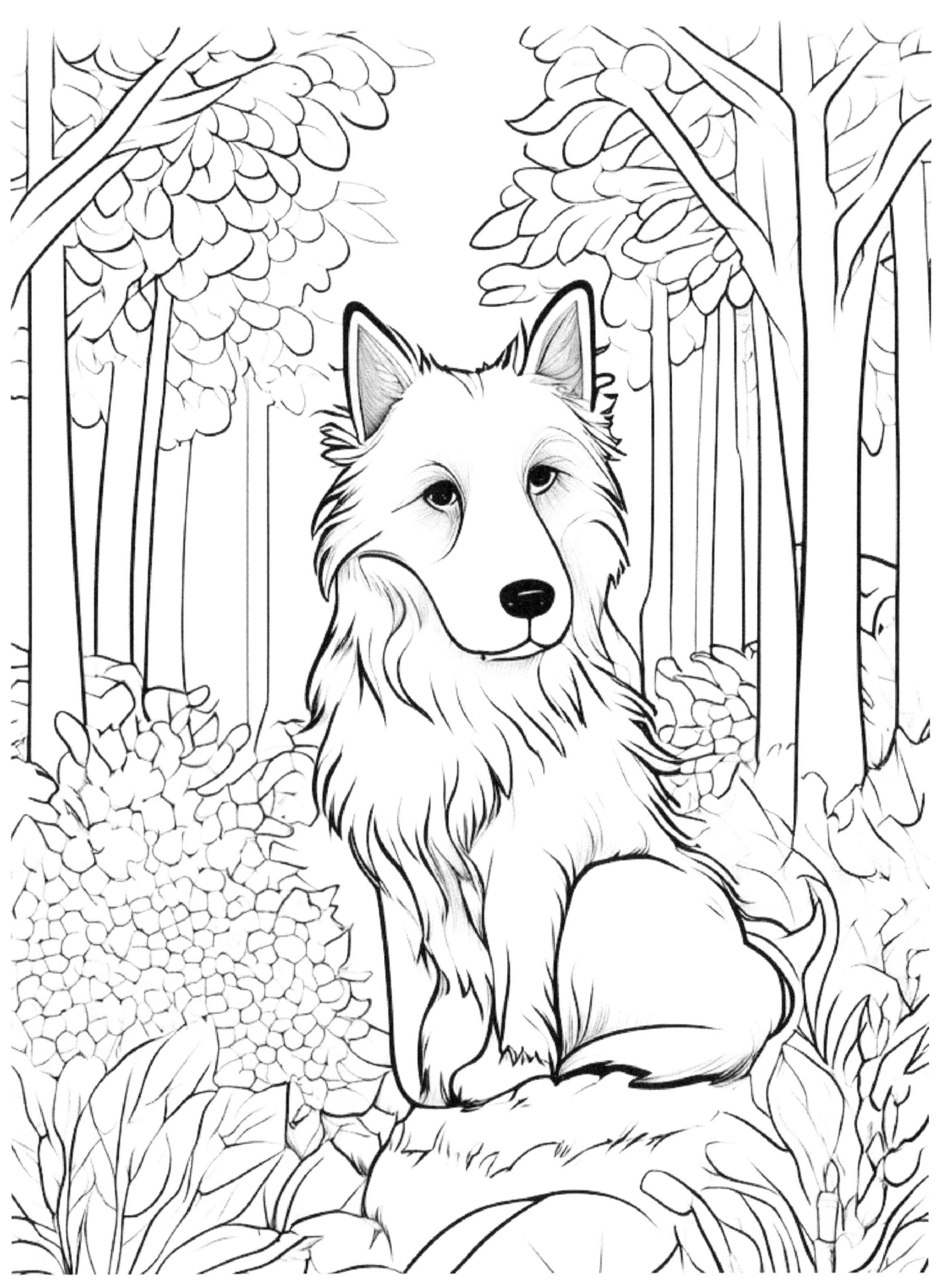

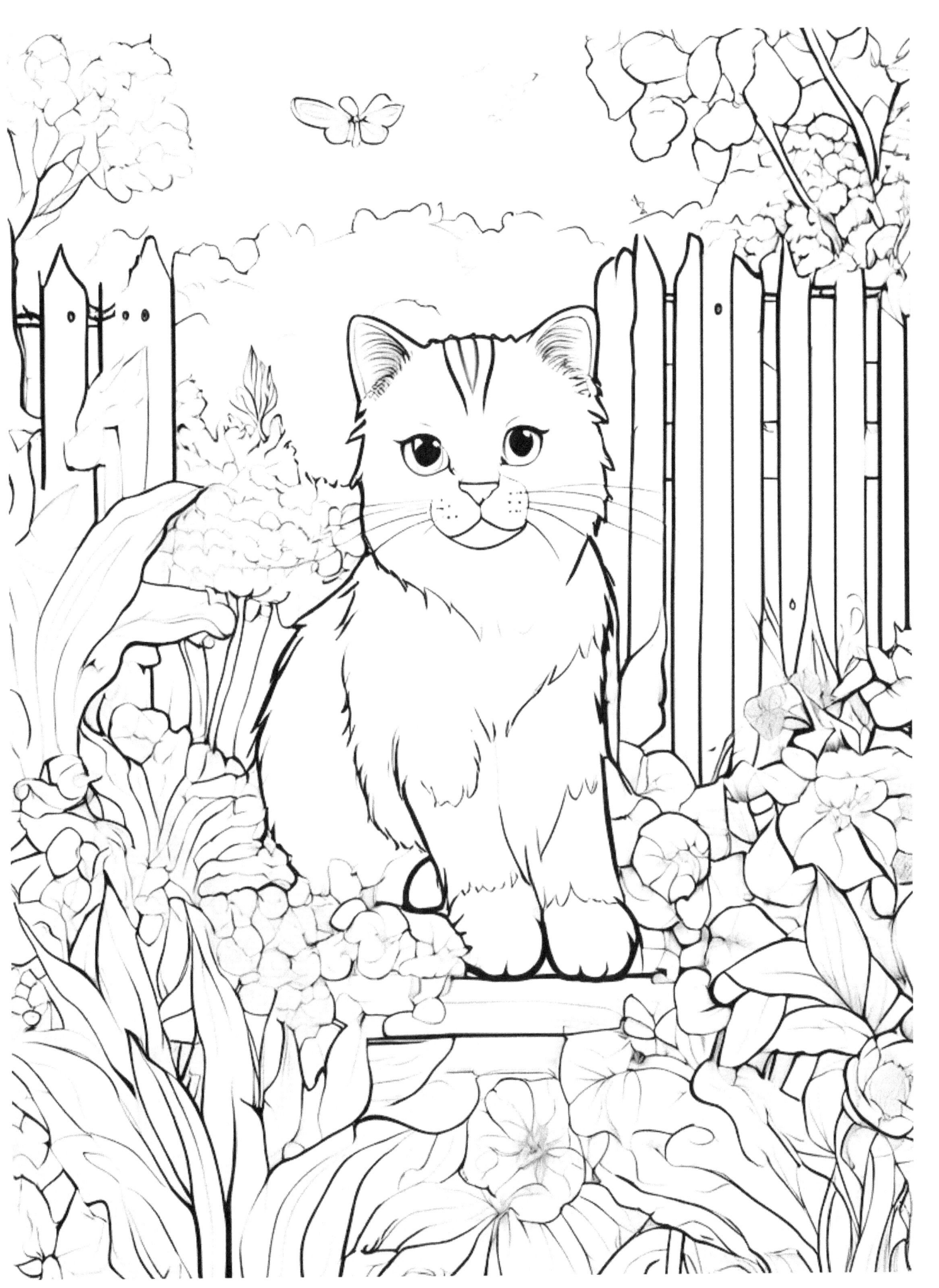

www.ingramcontent.com/pod-product-compliance
Lightning Source LLC
Chambersburg PA
CBHW062116220526
45471CB00010B/3761